ROUTLEDGE LIBRARY EDITIONS: AGING

Volume 25

AGEING, NEUROPSYCHOLOGY AND THE 'NEW' DEMENTIAS

AGEING, NEUROPSYCHOLOGY AND THE 'NEW' DEMENTIAS

Definitions, Explanations and Practical Approaches

UNA HOLDEN

LONDON AND NEW YORK

First published in 1995 by Chapman & Hall

This edition first published in 2024
by Routledge
4 Park Square, Milton Park, Abingdon, Oxon OX14 4RN

and by Routledge
605 Third Avenue, New York, NY 10158

Routledge is an imprint of the Taylor & Francis Group, an informa business

British Library Cataloguing in Publication Data
A catalogue record for this book is available from the British Library

ISBN: 978-1-032-67433-9 (Set)
ISBN: 978-1-032-72300-6 (Volume 25) (hbk)
ISBN: 978-1-032-72541-3 (Volume 25) (pbk)
ISBN: 978-1-032-72539-0 (Volume 25) (ebk)

DOI: 10.4324/9781032725390

Publisher's Note
The publisher has gone to great lengths to ensure the quality of this reprint but points out that some imperfections in the original copies may be apparent.

Disclaimer
The publisher has made every effort to trace copyright holders and would welcome correspondence from those they have been unable to trace.

Ageing, Neuropsychology and the 'New' Dementias

Definitions, explanations and practical approaches

Una Holden
Consultant clinical psychologist and freelance lecturer

CHAPMAN & HALL
London · Glasgow · Weinheim · New York · Tokyo · Melbourne · Madras

Published by Chapman & Hall, 2–6 Boundary Row, London SE1 8HN, UK

Chapman & Hall, 2–6 Boundary Row, London SE1 8HN, UK

Blackie Academic & Professional, Wester Cleddens Road, Bishopbriggs, Glasgow G64 2NZ, UK

Chapman & Hall GmbH, Pappelallee 3, 69469 Weinheim, Germany

Chapman & Hall USA, 115 Fifth Avenue, New York, NY 10003, USA

Chapman & Hall Japan, ITP-Japan, Kyowa Building, 3F, 2-2-1 Hirakawacho, Chiyoda-ku, Tokyo 102, Japan

Chapman & Hall Australia, 102 Dodds Street, South Melbourne, Victoria 3205, Australia

Chapman & Hall India, R. Seshadri, 32 Second Main Road, CIT East, Madras 600 035, India

Distributed in the USA and Canada by Singular Publishing Group Inc., 4284 41st Street, San Diego, California 92105

First edition 1995

Typeset in 10/12pt Palatino by Saxon Graphics Ltd, Derby
Printed in Great Britain by Page Bros, Norwich

ISBN 0 412 61340 9 1 56593 423 7 (USA)

A catalogue record for this book is available from the British Library

To my family,
colleagues and trainees

Contents

Preface

For many years my brain
Worked with a dim and undetermined sense
Of unknown modes of being.

WORDSWORTH

Until the last few years disturbances of brain function as explanations of strange or socially unacceptable behaviour were not considered or investigated.

Neuropsychological concepts were avoided by the majority of care staff as areas that were the province of particular professionals and of no relevance to their work. As more and more articles have appeared which relate specific behaviours to functional deficits, awareness has increased. Unfortunately such awareness is still limited and brain damage remains a subject that is rarely included in training programmes and all too often behavioural disturbances continue to be misunderstood, overlooked and misinterpreted. As a result of this omission in assessment and knowledge, goals can be set which are totally inappropriate, which are destined to fail or actually make matters more difficult for staff, relatives and patients.

Another topic which has suffered from vague discussion in staff training and has been presented in books and articles over the years with a variety of confusing explanations is the concept of dementia. At workshops and seminars, when participants are asked what they think the term means, the majority cite disturbed behaviour, progressive deterioration and possibly cell loss. They rarely have any definite ideas about the causes as often they believe dementia to be a disease in its own right.

In an earlier book, *Neuropsychology and Ageing* (Holden, 1988), some of the neuropsychological concepts and behaviours were discussed. Several of those chapters will be updated and included in this volume. However, other subjects have now become of equal relevance and chapters will be included to cover recent developments.

Most staff members need to know more about the recent research on conditions with which dementia is associated, with the many mistakes in diagnoses, including jumping to conclusions, overlooking acute confusion and the many normal changes with age that have not been taken into consideration when interpreting responses.

It is hoped that some gaps in knowledge and practice can be filled in – even a little – by the following chapters which are intended to clarify some of the terms, provide explanations and suggestions for simple and realistic assessments and outline some practical approaches to fairly common problems. Although neuropsychology is far from being a new field, there is still so much to learn and research continues to seek further explanations regarding the functions and nature of that remarkable machine called a brain. Many answers can be supplied by applying that rare commodity, common sense, but there is already sufficient available information on unusual behaviour due to brain damage to encourage awareness, to reconsider management practices and interventions in the light of their real value to an individual as well as to question assumptions and incomplete assessments.

Neuropsychology is the study of behaviour directly related to brain function. Although most people accept that psychological factors play a major role in influencing behaviour, the relevance of neuropsychological factors is rarely considered. Certain observed reactions, or lack of reactions, may be the result of brain damage rather than personality, mood, attitudes or affective disorders. To assume that specific behaviours have simple explanations could well obscure the real problems and needs. As previously stated, neuropsychology is not a new science; in fact man was aware of brain function in, at least, the 17th century BC. There is a papyrus dated from about 3000 BC on which accounts of head injury are recorded. Hippocrates, Aristotle, Galen and others from ancient times developed theories about the function and nature of the brain. Gall, amongst others, produced phrenological maps which can still be consulted in libraries. The late 19th century produced some of the classical contributors – Paul Broca and Carl Wernicke – who were followed in recent years by such eminent scientists as Aleksandr Romanovich Luria. Luria was one of the foremost authorities on restoration of function. His approaches are still used in practice and his work has been the inspiration for current researchers.

The role of a neuropsychologist includes:

- assisting in diagnosis;
- providing relevant assessment tools and methods;
- identifying methods to distinguish organic damage from functional states;

- monitoring change;
- identifying precipitants, e.g. effects of light on epilepsy;
- predicting outcome;
- assisting in the isolation and identification of new systems or pathways, syndromes or other aspects of brain-related behaviour;
- developing and assisting in rehabilitation and restoration of function programmes;
- counselling and supporting families;
- research.

This book is intended in particular for those who work with elderly people who have either no knowledge about neuropsychology or who have only a vague grasp of it. It is far from easy to produce something on a subject perceived as difficult that will prove attractive and informative reading for a wide variety of professions. Someone must try, though complete success with such a target is most unlikely; at least if some elderly people benefit, the effort will be worthwhile.

Una Holden-Cosgrove

REFERENCE

Holden, U.P. (ed.) (1988) *Neuropsychology and Ageing*. Croom Helm, London.

1

Recognizing the problem

We are all capable of misinterpreting human behaviour and language. Everyone is familiar with the problems faced in a doctor's surgery where both patient and physician struggle to get their message across to each other. The patient attempts to explain the pains, aches and feelings in a meaningful manner, and the doctor tries to make sense of all this in order to arrive at a correct diagnosis. Frequently both are frustrated by a perceived lack of understanding on the part of the other. Such a situation occurs every day in most interpersonal contacts. The stress is placed wrongly on a word, a gesture is misunderstood, someone deep in thought apparently ignores an acquaintance, a work situation appears threatening when it is only reflecting anxiety and a husband and wife relationship is put under duress because one or the other partner is tired. These upsets in personal relationships are commonplace and, to a degree, easy to appreciate. However, there are specific behaviours for which there does not appear to be a reasonable explanation and where even professionals are liable to error.

Mankind automatically explains perceptions according to experience, expectations, ability and knowledge. As all of these are essentially finite, errors frequently occur. People rarely stop to think, to examine the facts or to make further enquiry. Everyone is in a rush and too busy to pause. To spend valuable time on searching for alternatives interferes with the progress of work or interests and is regarded as a nuisance or too demanding. No one is genuinely willing to admit to ignorance, so when an unusual situation arises an answer has to be found quickly in order to avoid time wasting speculation.

Odd behaviour is viewed with some discomforture and often a pejorative remark will be used to dismiss the problem. If time to think was given to the situation alternative explanations would soon come to mind and could include:

- The person *is* really odd, a possible eccentric or local 'character'.
- The person could be socially naive or unskilled.
- There is a physical reason – delirium, amnesia, deafness, blindness.
- The problem is physiological – malnutrition, drug related, narcolepsy, etc.

- A psychiatric condition could be present.
- The person could have sustained a closed head injury.
- There could be specific neuropsychological deficits.

There are a whole series of situations where a person's behaviour can be misinterpreted and totally incorrect assumptions can lead to difficulties for all concerned. For instance, cognitive therapy highlights the classical situation by using as an example 'Mrs Jones' who is convinced her neighbour does not like her because she walked straight past her in the street. 'Mrs Jones' can be persuaded to look at many alternative explanations and think again. Her neighbour could have visual difficulties, she could have been deep in thought, thinking about a worrying or very happy experience. Hopefully, one of these suggestions proves correct, so 'Mrs Jones' can become more positive about herself and develop a different view of life. Sometimes the original negative perception proves to be correct and the unfortunate therapist is faced with a different problem!

An eccentric is accepted by society, but the person without social graces is not. It is rare that an individual falls into just one or the other of these categories. Normal people can present in many ways and their reactions may well be explained in a simple manner. Not everyone has perfect hearing or sight, old people in particular have experienced changes in their sensory ability.

At a club meeting Mrs Grant was in the middle of a group of six people discussing the local election. Mr Bell stated that he was absolutely disgusted at the idea that VAT should be placed on heating fuel. Mrs Grant, thinking that he was talking about a visit to a nearby distillery, lent forward and said 'Didn't you know that they closed down recently, so you wouldn't expect the vat to be full'. Everyone laughed at her so much that she refused to return to the club.

Normal changes in the senses can result in embarrassing situations and often the unfortunate individual who mishears or misperceives is so distressed by this that he or she will withdraw from social contact or become isolated in such a way as to suggest that some form of intellectual deterioration has taken place.

Kitwood (1990) has pointed out the importance of a person's background and environment as the most appropriate starting point in understanding a given behaviour. This will be discussed in more detail in Chapter 2, but here it is important to stress that many situations can result in giving false impressions. The older lady whose family insist on talking for her, the spouse whose partner has dominated life so much that he or she has withdrawn from arguments or even opinions or the individual whose life has been so full of tragedy that apathy has taken over, are all capable of providing examples of odd behaviour which can be misinterpreted only too easily.

It is surprising how rarely pejorative statements or erroneous explanations are challenged. The behaviour of those with a head injury and that of old people is invariably labelled, yet there are few who would question that label. Case notes contain word like 'aggressive', 'unmotivated' and 'violent', but the reason for the use of such strong words is not investigated. 'Incontinent' could mean that the person did not know where to find the toilet and could wait no longer. 'Aggression' could reflect a person's anger at being sat beside a patient who constantly swore, spat and interfered. 'Violent' might mean that a peacefully sleeping patient was suddenly awakened and laid hold of without warning by a staff member wanting to dress a wound. The possibility that the 'violent' reaction could be purely defensive has not been considered. When an account of preceeding events has not been recorded pejorative labels can result from false perspectives.

Neuropsychological factors are not understood by the general public. Care staff, too, can be ignorant of them. To some staff the words may be familiar, but the actual meaning or ability to recognize them remains vague. It is unfortunate that so many professionals are unsure of the subject as this vagueness ends in a lack of relevant treatment and understanding which can have tragic consequences for those with head injury and for older people in particular.

Geriatric wards and residential homes provide daily examples of misinterpreted behaviours and overlooked difficulties because staff are unaware of the possible implications. Table 1.1 lists some of the commoner behaviours and the probable conclusions drawn by staff and other observers.

Table 1.1 Examples of common behaviour and hasty assumptions

Observed behaviour	Assumption
Walking into things.	Forgetful. Blind.
Drops things, lacks dexterity.	Clumsy.
Gets into someone else's bed.	Over-sexed.
Complains of an assault.	Trouble maker.
Very slow. No response.	Unco-operative. Losing his/her mind.
Eats very little.	Anorexic. Apathetic.
Will not dress.	Unmotivated. Difficult.
Does not recognize faces or objects.	Blind. Apathetic.
Sings beautifully but will not talk.	Attention seeking. Stubborn.
Speech meaningless, silly words.	Totally deteriorated.
Forgets to pass on a message.	Senile.
Screams, pushes staff away when being dressed or fed.	Aggressive.

It is understandable if the public make false assumptions, particularly if there is no support system available to offer alternative explanations, but trained staff should all be aware that possibilities exist other than those which first spring to mind. There are many more situations apart from those in Table 1.1 and, obviously, many more explanations. In order to provide the most effective service it is imperative that a full assessment should be made of an individual when there is a possibility of organic damage and this cannot be done without a proper, trained, professional team.

In the new community care system in Great Britain there will be clients living at home who are being cared for by home helps and it is most important that they have access to both Social and Health Service teams, so that when a doubt arises early intervention is possible. The longer the delay the more difficult it will be to provide relevant assistance. To set goals for a client without covering all known possibilities is to court disaster. If staff have received at least some basic information regarding neuropsychological deficits the error factor could be considerably lessened. Even when such deficits are suspected there must be a means of involving appropriate professionals. The present concern about community care is the lack of good communication and co-operation between the different services involved.

TERMINOLOGY

Readers requiring a detailed account of neuropsychology should consult textbooks such as those by Walsh (1994) or Ellis and Young (1988). Most terms begin with an 'a' or 'dys'. The correct meaning of 'a' in this context is 'without' or 'lack of', and 'dys' means 'disordered'. In current practice these prefixes are used loosely, so that either can imply that a function is damaged or deficient.

Disorders of communication

Aphasia

Aphasia, or **dysphasia**, is a disturbance of language and includes speech, writing, reading and calculation. It is often used in relation to speech alone, though it should cover all forms of verbal communication. The dominant hemisphere of the brain – usually the left – is the main area responsible for language. Non-verbal communications, such as gesture, tone, rhythm and melody, are mainly controlled in the other hemisphere. So although a person may have difficulties in expressing or understanding verbal material, the *way* it is presented will be understood. Our gestures, the emphasis on words and the tone employed can convey meaning even though the actual words seem meaningless.

Agraphia, or **dysgraphia**, is a disturbance in writing and can vary in severity from a total inability to write to peculiar spelling, strangely formed letters or even small errors such as repeated or omitted letters or words. This is not due to a disability of the hand, arm or muscles, or to a lack of knowledge of how to write. Parkinson's disease and related conditions may interfere with writing ability, but the problem in these conditions is not due to an agraphia, but to the tremor.

Alexia, or **dyslexia**, refers to problems with reading. A person may have always had difficulty with understanding or making sense of the written word, or it may be that damage has occurred after learning to read.

Acalculia is difficulty with mathematics. Adding up, recognizing or writing numbers, calculating the cost of shopping, as well as handling more complicated mathematical problems are all to be considered under this term. The problem may have always been present (A calculia) or precipitated by a disease process or trauma (DYS calculia).

Amusia is an inability to understand, recognize or interpret music – melody, rhythm and tone are included here. Strictly speaking, amusia should not be included under the heading of aphasia as it is associated with damage in another part of the brain. However, because we all use emphasis and rhythm in our speech and because some patients with an aphasia are capable of singing although unable to converse, its inclusion here acts as a reminder that communication can take several forms, both verbal and non-verbal, and involve different areas of the brain.

The client's educational background must be investigated with all language disorders. Someone who never learned to read, write or to add cannot be expected to demonstrate such skills and could prove difficult to assess for language disabilities. It is also important to take intellectual ability levels into consideration.

Dysarthria is often mistaken for aphasia. It is frequently defined as imperfect articulation, as speech sounds so indistinct. However, there is much more involved than articulation. Impairments may be present in respiration, phonation, resonance, volume, rate, voice quality, intonation or rhythm. The person has no problem with word finding, sentence construction, expression of thoughts or any of the difficulties associated with a true aphasia, just with actual oral communication. To a listener the person sounds strange, gutteral, drunk, foreign or very quietly spoken. The dysarthria is due to a lesion in the upper or lower motor neurones, the basal ganglia or in the cerebellum, which results in weakness, paralysis or inco-ordination of the muscles and mechanisms associated with the larynx, pharynx or tongue.

It is important to note the differences between **language** and **speech**:

- Language: sounds, symbols, gestures; a learned and ordered system.
- Speech: actual production of words and the use of all the physical components to do so.

Linguistics is the transmission of messages in one particular language.

Language has four components:

- sounds: phonology/phonics;
- lexical system: vocabulary and gesture;
- grammar: syntax;
- meaning: semantic system.

Several terms are used to describe the different aspects of speech:

- Phonation: the basic system of speech necessary for the production of words.
- Articulation: actual production of speech.
- Phonemes: each separate sound. These sounds must be strung together to obtain meaning, i.e. ee/ff/ek/t = effect.
- Prosody: melodious aspect of speech which adds and clarifies meaning. For example the way the word 'great' can be emphasized to express size, importance or even the irritation experienced when a train has been missed.

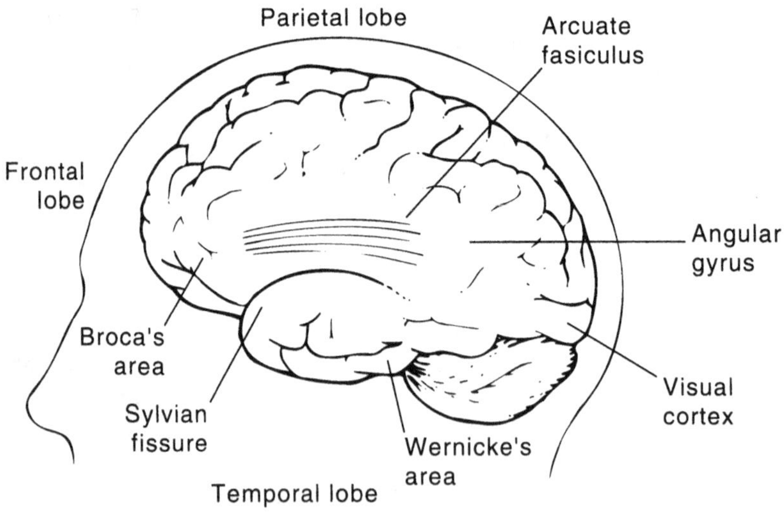

Figure 1.1 Brain Section

The process of speech requires the need to sort out thoughts, the meaning of incoming material and what verbal response is required. This is accomplished in the Wernicke's area – usually in the left dominant hemisphere involving the posterior part of the superior temporal gyrus (approximately where the left temporal lobe joins the frontal and parietal lobes, Figure 1.1). Here meaning is established, reponses and ideas are made sensible, pictorial or written material is converted into verbal components, answers are found to auditory input and then transmitted along the pathway (arcuate fasciculus) to the Broca's area in the posterior part of the frontal lobes (inferior frontal convolution). Providing that there is no malfunction, all the necessary expressive components are added in Broca's, the motor cortex is stimulated and speech is produced. This is greatly simplifying the process, but, in essence, this is what happens. So if there is damage in a particular part of this system different problems can arise.

Although man has much to learn about brain function (even language processes are not fully researched), speech impairment, as a result of damage to certain areas of the brain, has been recognized since at least 3000 BC. Paul Broca, in the mid-19th century, contributed enormously to the theories of localization of function and it was he who put forward the notion that speech was localized in the left hemisphere. About 12 years later Carl Wernicke, still only in his early twenties, added more detail to this contribution by delineating the posterior part of the superior temporal gyrus as the area concerned with comprehension.

Although disorders of language are quite numerous, two of the most commonly found in case notes are:

- **Broca's aphasia** which is also called expressive, non-fluent and motor. The usual area involved is the left dominant hemisphere, third frontal convolution.
- **Wernicke's aphasia** which is also referred to as receptive, fluent or sensory aphasia. The usual area involved is the left dominant hemisphere, posterior part of the superior temporal gyrus.

The features of Broca's aphasia are:

- No real comprehension difficulties.
- Anomia (word finding problems).
- Phonemes are mixed up, e.g. p for b, pelsil for pencil.
- Good automatic speech.
- Telegraphic agrammatism – omitted verbs, prefixes, etc. – key words only.
- Reading and writing are usually impaired.
- As insight is often present, frustration is common – the person can become angry or weepy.
- Speech is often awkward, hesitant or sparse.

- Some articulatory difficulties could be due to dyspraxia.
- Can name, but not repeat; comprehension is preserved so can read, but not aloud.
- Automatic phrase may be the only speech, e.g. 'Five, five, five', 'I don't know what to say', 'Hello/goodbye'.

Probably about 60–70% of aphasics are of this type.

The main features of Wernicke's aphasia are:

- Speech flows as there is usually no motor defect.
- Auditory comprehension is often damaged so incoming information is meaningless. Other people can be seen as crazy or as talking rubbish.
- Articulation is normal, but the person is paraphasic – uses the wrong word order in sentences, or the wrong word, e.g. match instead of lighter.
- Jargon, neologisms and meaningless verbalization are typical.
- Rhythm, stress and intonation are normal.
- Anomia (word finding), circumlocution (roundabout expression), perseveration (repetition) and echolalia (echoing) all occur.
- Insight is often lacking.
- Social responses are normal – understands expression, gesture and tone so picks up social cues.
- May laugh loudly and inappropriately – or weep.
- Could be verbally apraxic.
- Writing and reading are usually impaired.

There are a number of other important types of aphasia, including a global form which is most distressing for all concerned. An in depth account can be found by Thompson, in Holden (1988) or by Murdoch (1990). Table 1.2 provides some details of the differing types of aphasia.

Table 1.2 A classification of aphasic syndromes with symptoms (Thompson, in Holden, 1988)

Name of aphasia	Site of lesion	Symptoms
Motor (Broca's) aphasia	Left pre-motor area	Cannot move from one sound to another in a word. Speech loses automatic fluency and becomes fragmented and tense. Telegraphic speech may occur with recovery. Melodic structure may go. Difficulty in transition complicated by lack of inhibition. Writing reflects speech pattern: perseveration of word once written.
Sensory (Wernicke's) aphasia	Posterior third superior temporal gyrus	Cannot distinguish, isolate identify or repeat phonemes.

Table 1.2 continued

		Cannot understand speech; uses jargon, automatisms. Cannot name objects. Cannot read or recognize letters. Can copy but not write spontaneously. Retains functions of visual perception, prosody, logicogrammatical relationships and calculation. Cannot respond to prompting of first sound or syllable. Reduced awareness of errors.
Acoustic-amnestic aphasia	Inferior temporal lobe	Phonemic hearing only slight disturbance. Audioverbal memory damaged. Cannot retain series of sounds, syllables or words. Can produce short series of successive stimuli given after interval. Tends to give last given stimulus. Cannot recall words. Frequently can write series.
Semantic (nominal) aphasia	Posterior parietal-occipital lobe	Cannot name objects, less difficulty with verbs and adjectives. Cannot recall clear visual image of object to be named. Immediate response to cue of initial sound or syllable. Often confuses words from same semantic category. Paraphasia. Understands individual words but logicogrammatical relationships disturbed. Inability to see parts in relation to whole. Spatial and temporal relations disturbed. Acalculia. Difficulty in making letters and finding spatial directions. Retained intonation and melodic structure.
Articulatory dyspraxia	Left central region	Cannot assume correct lip, tongue, etc., position due to difficulty in finding particular articuleme. Writing and read ing aloud difficult. Substitutions of phonemes similar in place and manner of production e.g. t/d, 1/r, p/m/b.
Dynamic aphasia	Left inferior pre-frontal region	Lacks spontaneity of speech, cannot initiate or sustain long

Table 1.2 continued

	passage of speech. No dialogue, unable to retell story or give picture description. Can repeat words and short sentences, can be echolalic, cannot alter order. Can initiate novel answer if given visual cue. Writing can be grammatically accurate, but meaningless. Poor awareness of errors.

It is important to stress that every individual suffering from a language disorder will probably have a unique problem. Not only can a lesion occur anywhere along the language pathways in the dominant hemisphere (i.e. in Wernicke's, in the arcuate fasiciculus or in Broca's), but damage can occur in the passage of information across from one hemisphere to another. Furthermore, personality, intelligence, experience and acquired knowledge vary from person to person and the resultant problems will differ accordingly.

The effects of specific disease processes are another matter again. Damage caused by a stroke, tumour, head injury or organic disease will differ and so it is vital to establish the cause before coming to any conclusion about the nature of the problem or the way to treat or manage it. The complications that are often associated, e.g. dysgraphia, alexia or dyscalculia, can assist the diagnosis and to some extent localization, so it is important to note and record all variations in individual language disturbances.

Emotional responses to an aphasia should be noted as well. Some patients are severely affected, whilst others may simply appear to hesitate or to be slow or not very mentally agile. In some cases, contact with others may be profoundly disturbed, particularly when good oral communication is impossible, or when the effects are so intense that the person seems to be psychotic. Mildly impaired people can become increasingly anxious in company as they are aware of their errors and hesitations, and may be so embarrassed by them that they avoid the social scene entirely and increase their difficulties by lack of practice and limited success.

Disorders of movement

Apraxia

This term refers to a series of movement disorders. It indicates an impairment of voluntary and purposeful movements which is not caused by limb, muscle or mechanism weakness or defect, nor is it due to lack of comprehension. The person is quite capable of performing the action and will do so automatically. The individual may fully appreciate what to do, but the moment the movement comes under conscious control will experience difficulties. The organization and co-ordination of thought and appropriate action are not operating effectively. The motor mechanic who has taken cars apart and put them back again for many years begins to replace a new part and suddenly finds that he cannot work out what goes where. The lady who has won prizes for her knitting suddenly discovers that she cannot make a purl stitch when asked to demonstrate one. The disorder is quite common, but is frequently misinterpreted. The principal forms of apraxia are ideomotor, ideational, constructional, dressing, verbal and buccofacial.

Ideomotor apraxia Here a person is incapable of performing a simple, single gesture. Automatically he or she will wave 'Goodbye', pick up something, or make an often used gesture. The moment attention is drawn to such an action the ability to perform it appears to vanish. A Catholic will regularily make the sign of the cross in prayer; when asked to make this sign the person will not know where to start. Understanding is present, but the memory for the pattern of performance has been lost in some way. Response by imitation can be at a better level. Behavioural responses can vary from client to client, for example there may be many movements or none at all in attempting tasks.

Ideational apraxia Here the individual is incapable of carrying out a complex task involving a series of movements. Order and sequencing are lost once the action is under voluntary control, and a task which normally is performed with ease becomes a traumatic experience and completely disordered. The plan or engram is preserved but the ability to extract the overall plan with its correct sequence has been lost. Understanding is present, the person knows what is required but is unable to perform the movements in the right order. The classical example is to ask the person to take a match from a box, strike it and light a candle. The instructions are comprehended, the individual is a smoker who lights matches throughout the day, but when asked to do so becomes thoroughly confused. The matches drop on the floor, the candle can be rubbed on the box instead of the matches – the result is total chaos. As with ideomotor apraxia, patients' behavioural responses vary. The patient may stop trying after the first error, may make a different action altogether or may add more and more actions which confuse the response even further. Sometimes imitation can assist a correct response.

In acute cases the observer will notice that the patient's hands are so stiffly bent that they resemble a bunch of bananas! The person tries hard to loosen and use the fingers, but they become stiffer and all movement of the hands and arms become rigid or even choreiform. The moment action and movement return to non-voluntary status, hands and arms look and perform normally.

Arguments continue over the relationship between ideomotor and ideational apraxia; there are differences of opinion about the location of lesions and the extent of damage. Although both are often associated with the parietal lobes, different researchers suggest other areas, bilaterality or no localization at all. Such arguments and more detailed discussion of the apraxias can be obtained from textbooks and articles on neuropsychology. Here, in order to improve understanding of an individual's behavioural responses, the emphasis is on improving and discussing awareness, the practical aspects, the need for relevant tests and the need to take such possible disorders into consideration in rehabilitation programmes.

Constructional apraxia The presence of constructional apraxia is not easy to establish simply by observation. It may be suggested by apparent difficulties in spatially manipulating things, e.g. assembling mechanisms, or objects, even putting a jigsaw together. To obtain as much information about its nature as possible some tests should be employed. Often the patient cannot put parts together to make a whole; on other occasions no parts are correctly joined or constructed. Right hemisphere damage to the parietal or tempero-parietal lobes produces visuo-spatial impairments for which a model to copy will not prove helpful – in fact it can increase the person's confusion. When damage has occurred in the left parietal or tempero-parietal region, models or cues can be of assistance. For instance, if the block designs from the Wechsler Intelligence Test are used (using coloured blocks to make pictured designs), the pictures can help those with left-sided damage so that, at least up to a point, the cubes can be correctly placed to achieve the pattern required, though eventually problems will arise in placing the last cube. In the case of a person with right-sided damage, the cubes will not be joined together and will be spread in a straight line or even built into towers bearing no resemblance whatsoever to the pattern on the picture. Providing cues for those with non-dominant parietal or tempero-parietal damage only adds to their confusion. Present theory suggests a motor defect as a result of left hemisphere lesions, so there is an inability to establish a programme for the correct action, and in the case of right hemisphere damage there is a defect in the person's ability to perceive spatial relationships.

Dressing apraxia This appears to be related to lesions in the non-dominant parietal and occipital areas. In most cases the well learned, almost automatic system for dressing oneself has been lost. The relationship of clothes to person is not apparent to the patient. True dressing apraxia is probably separate from one-sided neglect, where the person dresses one side of the body and not the other. Dressing apraxia is bi-lateral and can also be associated with a figure–ground disturbance so that the clothes and the place on which they lie cannot be dissociated from each other. This is another visuo-spatial defect and the degree of deficit varies from person to person.

Not all of those who have problems with dressing have this disorder – there are those old ladies who for many other reasons will sit and wait until someone helps them to dress. There are many reasons for this behaviour – a belief that staff are paid to do this, a fear of not conforming to the rules, a wish for attention or staff needs to complete tasks as quickly as possible are some of the explanations. However, dressing apraxia is a fairly common problem and should always be considered when apparent dressing problems arise. The engram, or plan for dressing, has been lost and the right movements to associate clothes with person cannot be found. Another possibility is that the person has lost the ability to reverse or rotate things in space. Many people have difficulty with reading mirror writing or reading things upside down. To demonstrate how common this is, a group of 'normal' people facing a lecturer can be asked to draw something, e.g. sticks with different coloured ends formed into a particular shape, as the lecturer sees them, rather than as they see them. Errors in reversal are not uncommon. When trying to dress it is necessary to reverse many pieces in order to dress correctly. If the person has lost the ability to see how objects can be reversed in space he or she will have difficulties with dressing.

Buccofacial and other apraxias There are a number of other types of apraxia – whole-body, gait disturbances, loss of ability to sing, whistle or hum, other effects on language and even the buccofacial loss of voluntary movements of the tongue, mouth and other parts of the face. The patient blows, sucks, puffs the cheeks and sticks out his or her tongue with ease until requested to perform that action. The ability to wink, raise eyebrows and wiggle the nose are also lost under voluntary control. Speech therapists provide treatment programmes for patients who have developed an apraxia for speech.

Agnosia

Agnosia is an inability to recognise sensory perceptions which is not due to a defect in the sensory system concerned, ignorance of the nature of the object, sound, taste, smell or feel, to defective intelligence or to acute confusion. This condition is infrequently identified, almost impossible to observe and the subject of much neuropsychological study. The visual form is the commonest.

Visual or object agnosia

This is not only the inability to name or demonstrate the use of an object without touching it, but also a total lack of recognition of the object's meaning or character. The person does not even remember seeing anything like it before. In some cases a good logical mind can pick up clues to advantage, in others the structuring of shapes becomes a major problem.

The disorder is frequently misinterpreted as being related to language or visual memory problems. However, if another sense is used to aid identification, meaning usually becomes apparent. A simple test is to ask the patient to name, by sight alone, a simple object such as a lipstick case. The shape, colour and perhaps the notion that it is a container are the most likely responses. Once able to handle and examine it, an answer usually follows quickly. The condition is rare, and as such provokes much argument as to the location of the lesion and the nature of the disability. The right occipital region is frequently mentioned; some authors suggest lesions are in the left occipital region and the splenium (part of the corpus callosum, the fibres of which connect with both hemispheres), others consider it to be a visuo-verbal disconnection syndrome. Whatever its true location – and it differs from individual to individual anyway – it is associated with strokes, tumours, head injuries and some conditions with which a dementia is present. Its presence has implications for management programmes.

Two other rare and interesting variations of visual agnosia are **prosopagnosia** and **simultanagnosia.**

Prosopagnosia is an inability to recognize familiar faces, often including the person's own face. Relatives can be upset by finding that they are seen as strangers, or a parent instead of a spouse. It is not unknown for a man to accuse his wife of infidelity because he keeps seeing a 'strange man' in his mirror. Obviously women can suffer from the same illusion. Sometimes this disorder is the only presenting difficulty, sometimes it is one of many. It occurs after strokes, with tumours, head injury and often with dementia. Lesions appear to be related to the right occipital region, but many factors must be considered as the explanation or even psychiatric state will vary from person to person.

Simultanagnosia is an inability to see a whole configuration as each part of that whole becomes the focus of attention. The problem is one of synthesis or of visual fixation. In Balint's syndrome for instance (refer to Chapter 5) a person has difficulty with scanning, a form of apraxia of vision, and once he or she fixes on a part of an object or picture is incapable of moving on to take in the rest of it. Each part, often a tiny part, will be clearly identified, but the whole thing will not. Similarly, a whole series of moving pictures will prove meaningless, but one of the still pictures will make sense. Pictures presented on a complicated background or obscured in some way will cause great confusion and highlight the disability. There can be further problems in reading words, which are often perceived one letter at a time. Once again, though the occipital lobe seems to be the damaged area, there could be a language problem as well and involvement of several systems rather than just one location.

Auditory, or acoustic, agnosia

This very rare state is demonstrated when a person fails to recognize either speech or sound, or both. Acoustic agnosia usually refers to non-verbal sounds and lesions in the right hemisphere. If the lesion is in the auditory association area of the left hemisphere, receptive aphasia results. With auditory agnosia the person has difficulty in distinguishing between similar phonemes, e.g. 'p' and 'b'. In other words there is a problem with auditory discrimination. To the afflicted person speech may sound like an unfamiliar foreign language or nonsense talk. Surprisingly when the other person slows down the rate of speech there is no longer a difficulty in comprehension. Problems in identifying unseen noises can occur at the same time as speech ones, or may occur on their own. There are obvious dangers for the person with auditory agnosia for sounds – honking horns, warning sirens or other sounds indicating danger may prove meaningless unless the person can see from whence they come. Deafness as well as blindness must be excluded before concluding an agnosic state is present.

Spatial agnosia

This is mainly an inability to find the way around, even in familiar places – a disorientation for space. The person may be able to recognize familiar objects, but has problems in identifying even the rooms in his or her own home and 'forgets' where things are kept. Maps can also prove useless. A flight navigator, after sustaining a moderately severe stroke, found that he was no longer capable of making sense of his charts, and was considerably relieved that as he recovered this skill returned. It is not unusual to find a driver who, whilst on holiday in a strange area, develops some disability, probably a mini stroke (or transient ischaemic attack – TIA), and is suddenly incapable of following the planned route. Strokes, head injuries, tumours, TIAs and dementia-related conditions, amongst other disorders, are capable of producing this unwelcome experience. Loss of topographical memory, visual field defects, difficulties with three dimensions and the spatial manipulation of objects are only some of the difficulties that are considered to fall under this heading. The right hemisphere and the occipital lobes are much favoured as the sites of lesions, but other parts of the brain – particularly the frontal lobes – must be suspect in the individual case.

Colour agnosia

Colour agnosia is an important indicator of damage to the occipital region. There are two forms of colour agnosia. First a difficulty in identifying colours in daily living. Matching, selecting deeper or lighter shades or even sorting colours prove extremely difficult or impossible. The person is not colour blind, tests such as the Ishihara (used in selecting pilots during the Second World War) show colour vision is normal. In the second type, colour naming is impaired. Once again colour tests are normal, but the person is unable to name colours or recognize the name when it is supplied.

The first type of colour disorder is probably related to right hemisphere damage and the latter more related to dysphasia. Usually other symptoms and signs can be found which help to provide a better picture of the individual problem.

Disorders of taste and smell

Disorders of these senses, although of great nuisance value to individuals, have received little attention from research as they are not regarded as priorities. Taste and smell are closely linked and are affected by the ageing process. Sensory acuity does change over time and men are more prone to lose the sense of smell than women. Older people often complain that food does not taste as good as it used to taste, or even that something tastes 'poisonous'. This is due to the changes in the sense of smell which usually makes the food more appealing. Awareness of these changes can help carers to understand some of the complaints.

Astereognosis

This condition is also called tactile agnosia. Here the person is unable to recognize objects by touch alone. It is hard to distinguish this from sensory weakness of the hand which is probably made more intense if arthritis or other related conditions are present. Shape discrimination is possibly the most relevant aspect of tactile disorder, and is mainly caused by right hemisphere lesions. Practically, astereognosis poses added problems for the old and frail. Finding keys in the dark, searching for money in a pocket or handbag are all anxiety provoking or potentially embarrassing situations.

Home helps and other visitors could encourage their clients to find safe and easier ways to identify important objects that they cannot recognize by touch alone. As shape appears to be the main defect and texture and roughness could well be preserved, something rough could be attached to the house key and weight could be used to identify coins. Another aid would be a small torch with an easily identifiable casing or in a well learned place – for example the only thing in that particular pocket. As long as the person can see, the object will be easily identified.

Somatognosis

Somatognosis refers to body image disturbances. There are a considerable number of terms which fall under this heading and only a brief mention of some of them will be made here:

- Micrognosia: perceiving body parts as smaller than they are.
- Macrognosia: perceiving body parts as larger than they are.
- Finger agnosia: unable to point to or show fingers when asked to do so. This condition is part of the classical Gerstmann syndrome, which will be discussed later.
- The phantom limb is an experience which can occur after a limb amputation – the person feels that the lost limb is still attached.

There are many other body image disturbances which are not relevant in this context, those interested in more detail should consult Heilman, Valenstein and Watson (1985).

Unilateral visual inattention

Other terms for this are unilateral asomatognosias (rarely used) and simply the neglect syndrome. Neglect of one side of the body primarily affects the left side in right-handed people with right hemisphere lesions. Exceptions to this are rare and probably only right dominant hemisphere people have neglect to the right side and they are quite rare anyway. The condition can take several forms, though all may be present:

- Unilateral spatial neglect, where patients will fail to see anything to their left and bump into things, fail to see food on the other side of the plate or ignore one side of a page when reading.
- Hemi-inattention, where the person is unable to report on stimuli presented to the neglected side.
- Sensory inattention, where the person cannot distinguish when a stimulus is applied to the neglected part of the body.
- Anosognosia is denial of damage or denial of the damaged part of the body. Patients will ignore a paralysed limb or deny that it is theirs; sometimes they will not even try to dress that side of their body.

Unilateral neglect is far from uncommon and is frequently found with stroke patients, though not exclusively so. All sensory input to that side will be ignored – even talking to the patient from the wrong side will not elicit a response. The right parietal lobe is the area most commonly affected; hemipareisis is usually, but not always, present. It can also occur with frontal damage and also with some sub-cortical lesions. The acute form will lessen in a matter of weeks, but some signs will persist.

Other factors

Certain forms of unusual behaviour can also be closely associated with particular areas of the brain. One factor that should always be considered is **laterality**. It is important, particularly with older people, to establish handedness. Many left-handers were taught to use the right hand at school and when a change has taken place in brain function errors can result from assuming that a patient is a true right-hander.

Areas such as the frontal, parietal and sub-cortical play major roles in explanations of unusual behaviour. The slowness, apathy and apparent forgetfulness of a person with a sub-cortical condition can be overlooked and incorrect management procedures can be initiated. The often aggressive and impulsive behaviour of a person with frontal damage can lead to police involvement.

Because patients with a sub-cortical condition respond so slowly it is assumed that they are intellectually and globally deteriorating. The presence of a dysarthria is often mistaken for a dysphasia and the absence of any true aphasia, agnosia or apraxia remains unnoticed. Although slowed down or dilapidated intellectually, patients with sub-cortical states remain intellectually able until very late in the disease process. If an able person is treated as someone without any ability he or she will succomb to anxiety and depression and deterioration may well be encouraged. Impatient responses or reactions will affect motivation. Such patients will frequently reply 'I don't know' when questioned – they are aware of the impatience and use this response as a defence against the dismissiveness of others. Such patients require support, time and a higher level of expectation. Sub-cortical conditions will be discussed in more detail in Chapter 4.

The effects of damage to the frontal regions are remarkable enough to be named the **frontal lobe syndrome**. Personality changes are marked and even in the very young can result in unsociable and unacceptable behaviour (refer to Chapter 2). Frontal damage can occur for a variety of reasons, e.g. head injury, tumour or organic conditions. Each case will present in a different way and perhaps only some of the signs listed in Table 1.3 will be present, but in severe cases most of them will be found.

Parietal lobe damage can also cause notable changes in certain behaviours, especially those involving spatial relationships. There is a need to investigate carefully the possibility of damage if a person has difficulty in finding the way, shows signs of body image disturbance or has difficulties in construction. Disorders of agraphia, acalculia, finger agnosia and right/left disorientation suggest left parietal damage and are commonly collected together under the term Gerstmann syndrome, which will be discussed in more detail in Chapter 2.

Table 1.3 Frontal damage signs

Garrulous, flow of thought and speech excessive.
Perseveration, repeating words, phrases or ideas. Can also occur in writing, drawing and visual tasks.
'Stuck needle' syndrome – will become fixed on an event, an idea, etc. Unable to change 'set'.
Logical thinking damaged.
Impulsivity, can do or say the first thing in mind.
Abstract thought damaged. May find it hard to assess own behaviour or responses and feelings of others. Creativity may be impaired.
Sequencing impaired, order has been lost, cannot perform tasks or complete movements in right order.
Judgement and planning are disordered.
Personality may change, could be aggressive or apathetic.

Elderly people

As this book is concerned with elderly people the relevance of neuropsychology to this age group must be considered. In many instances the clients in care are frail and ill, so often standard test procedures prove unsuitable and undesirable. However, it must be stressed that a proper investigation is vital in each case in order to provide logical and sensible grounds for treatment or management programmes. The actual process of investigation will be outlined in Chapter 2, but it is important to recognize the need to obtain as much relevant information about a person as possible. Whilst there are many who will resent, reject or be unable to respond to formal testing, and therefore less stressful measures should be employed, not all older people are frail and incapable of coping with the more formal examinations. The majority of over 65s are fit, well and independent and able to respond to demanding situations. Older people who attend general medical clinics are frequently very capable and, if treated with respect and allowed to keep their dignity, will be able to cope with investigations as well as any other age group.

In our eagerness to protect a group from exploitation and embarrassment it remains as important to avoid over-protectiveness and patronization as it is to put them under undue stress and unnecessary threat. It is not unusual to discover that the client aged 90 years is more intellectually able than the examiner!

ALTERNATIVE EXPLANATIONS OF OBSERVED BEHAVIOUR

In this chapter the aim is to suggest more careful assessments. All investigations regarding older people need an initial common sense approach. So far the discussion has been concerned with defining neuropsychological concepts, but these possibilities should never be the first step in clarifying the cause of unusual or changed behaviour. An initial enquiry should carefully exclude 'normal' influences.

Has the person had a traumatic experience? Are other people taking over his or her life to such an extent that the person has just withdrawn and allowed dependency to develop? Has the person always tended to be domineering and now is making more demands on those outside the family? These are just some of the questions that require an answer **before** even thinking about a physical or organic disorder.

An assessment should include social and environmental backgrounds, normal changes due to ageing rather than impairment, skills, daily living activities and routines, patterns of behaviour, previous levels of cognitive functioning as well as the current performance and interests and abilities. Then the physical state and also identification of brain function abilities and impairments should be examined. Without such an overall picture mistakes will be made, misinterpretations will occur and improper programmes and goals will be created. Apart from overlooking environmental and normal ageing effects, some of the commonest errors are in misinterpreting behaviour which may well be related to some form of neuropsychological deficit.

The behaviours listed in Table 1.4 are in a simplified form and require further thought. Walking into things usually implies some form of visual impairment. However, there are many other possibilities, some of these are obvious – blindness, thinking about something else, 'miles away', delirium, limb weakness. Others are not so well known. Strokes, tumours and head injuries can produce body image disturbance such as anosognosia. If an object is on the neglected side of the body the patient will not be aware of it and so will walk into it. The rare Balint's Syndrome (refer to Chapter 3), where the patient has a fixation of gaze, an optic ataxia and impaired visual attention, could be the reason for regular accidents. Patients with progressive supranuclear palsy (Chapter 5) suffer from stiffness and an inability to lower their eyes and so are most likely to trip over objects they cannot see; for them walking, reading, writing and eating cause immense problems.

Dexterity deficits are rarely pure clumsiness. Tremors, shakes and stiffness should be noted and the possibility of a TIA must be investigated. A Parkinson tremor and the slowness of response of this and other subcortical states provide a good explanation for clumsiness and apparent lack of motivation and co-operation.

Table 1.4 Examples of behaviours and possible alternative explanations

Observed behaviours	Alternative explanations to be investigated
Walks into things.	Visual problems. Weakness due to stroke. Alcoholism, tumour, head injury, Anosognosia. Autotopagnosia.
Drops things, lacks dexterity.	Parkinson's disease, peripheral weakness, apraxia, stroke.
Inappropriate laughing or crying.	Possible frontal lesion.
Get's into someone else's bed, complains of assault.	Probably unilateral neglect, anosognosia.
Very slow, little response.	Depression, sub-cortical state.
Eats very little.	Normal habit. Anorexia. Peripheral field problem. Anosognosia.
Will not dress.	Dressing apraxia. Agnosia, anosognosia.
Fails to recognize faces or objects.	Probably visual agnosia and prosopagnosia.
Will not speak, sings beautifully.	Amusia centre spared, stroke caused dysphasia.
Says nothing or uses nonsense words.	Probably dysphasic.
Forgets to pass on message.	Probably suffering from benign forgetfulness, just like anyone else!

Errors in appreciating language impairments are widespread. Few people are aware that, although language is essentially the concern of the dominant hemisphere (usually the left), music, melody, rhythm and tempo are usually sited in the other hemisphere. As a result the 'singer' with dysphasia for speech is often regarded as a malingerer. Sadly a number of composers – Ravel for example – have suffered tragically from amusia. Their speech was preserved but their musical ability was damaged. Amusic patients have varied difficulties; some hear music in their heads but cannot write, play or sing it, others hear a cacophanous noise rather than a melody. As disability can affect the daily work and pleasure of ordinary people it can also affect creative and imaginative minds, causing much suffering and loss unless suitable support is offered and further research with rehabilitation in focus is encouraged.

It is advisable, but not always possible, to call in the help of a neuropsychologist, speech therapist or occupational therapist in order to clarify the problem. Outside neurology few medical specialties are conversant with neuropsychology and as a result important aspects of behaviour are overlooked. It is vital to the patient that his or her observed behaviour is understood and allowance made for it in all rehabilitation or management programmes. Simple screening tests are possible and some knowledge of neuropsychological concepts is preferable to total ignorance. Common sense and basic knowledge are reasonable tools. Staff can examine the situation for themselves by making careful enquiries, observations of behaviour and by careful recording. Essentially basic neuropsychology should be more widely included in staff training.

Regular discussion and consideration of the questionable behaviours and their possible causes would be the proper sequel to an observation period. During this time all retained abilities, no matter how basic, should be recorded. A good starting point could be 'does the patient breathe?'. The question comes as a shock, at first amusing, but it prompts recall of quite basic positive examples of skills and abilities as well as positive aspects of the patient's personality. The great rush to set targets based on initial and probably faulty information should be discouraged. A delay, during which all the patient receives is TLC, will do more to assist rehabilitation and provide a better opportunity to assess retained and impaired function than an impressive looking, worthless set of goals.

Case 1

Mrs Annie Greer was 82 years old. She had lost her husband two years ago and had become so distressed that she was persuaded to sell her home and go to live with her daughter. The daughter complained that she was no longer capable of caring for herself. She stated that Mrs Greer would not talk to anyone, sat in her chair all day, was washed and dressed by the daughter and, although she could eat by herself, would do nothing to help with preparing the meals or do any housework. When staff members tried to ask her questions the daughter always provided the answers. It proved extremely difficult to spend time alone with the patient, either the daughter or her husband were always in attendence. Mrs Greer offered no response and simply sat and stared into space.

In order to obtain a proper assessment and understanding of the situation arrangements were made to bring Mrs Greer into the Day Hospital. A remarkable change took place! Within a matter of days it became obvious that it was the daughter who had the problem not the mother. When on her own the lady proved perfectly capable of answering questions and responding to a social situation, in fact she revelled in it! She began to take an interest in her appearance, wanted to help prepare the tables for meals and chattered to everyone. It was only when further enquiries were made that the real story became clear.

Mrs Greer was dreadfully upset by her husband's death. Her daughter wanted to help and took over all arrangements and care of her mother to such an extent that Mrs Greer was left with nothing to do except sit and grieve about her loss. Before she knew what was happening, decisions were made for her, she was regimented as to when she should rise and retire and what she should do. Her daughter spoke for her on every occasion. As she was always inclined to be rather passive in nature she did not have the courage to tell her daughter to back away and retired into her shell as a defence. A few sessions of counselling with the daughter and her husband resulted in a much changed situation and Mrs Greer obtained a warden controlled flat with a good social atmosphere for herself.

From this example it is possible to see how easy it could be to accept the situation as it was presented. It would be very easy to conclude that Mrs Greer was deteriorating, or had a depression, and treat her accordingly. She was probably depressed, but the depression would only have been due to circumstances capable of change. Her bereavement was natural, but her opportunities to cope with it were limited by a well meaning, over-protective daughter. Retiring into her shell and withdrawing from an unpleasant, undemanding situation was the only answer that a non-assertive person could find.

Case 2

The nurses on a geriatric ward were deeply distressed when Mr Brown and his relatives threatened court action. They claimed that he had been assaulted by one of the night staff. This was vigorously denied and both staff and relatives anxiously sought clarification of the incident.

Mr Brown had suffered a severe stroke which had paralysed his left arm. Ten days after the event he was still extremely impaired intellectually and unable to do much for himself. He was capable of finding his way to the toilet at night, but upset the other patients by climbing into bed with another patient on his return. In many ways Mr Brown was far from popular because of this.

When further investigations were instigated it became clear that he had an anosognosia and unilateral neglect. As a result he completely ignored his left side, made no response to any stimuli or anybody on that side and even insisted that his left arm did not belong to him.

The most likely explanation for the reported incidents was that he could see the toilet to his right side, but on his return his bed was situated on his neglected left, so he was unable to see it and got into bed approximately where it should be. The assault could be explained by appreciating that during the night when he turned over in bed the part of his body that he accepted as his own came into contact with the arm that he claimed was not his. Logically if there is an arm in the bed that is not part of the person lying there, it must belong to someone else who had no right to be there!

When this possibility was demonstrated to the relatives and staff they were surprised to learn of the existence of such a condition and convinced by the explanation. Although the staff were exceedingly well trained and very caring, they had failed to recognize the connection between unilateral neglect and the reported incidents. Mr Brown's denial of his arm had been noted, some of the neglect had also been observed, but no mention of this had been written in the case notes. If the good training had also included basic neuropsychological concepts this situation might not have occurred.

Case 3

Mrs Black was causing concern amongst the residential home care staff. Since her admission 12 months previously she had been gradually deteriorating. Now she appeared unmotivated, unco-operative and very clumsy. She was so messy at mealtimes that they found it easier to feed her themselves. Mornings and evenings were made more demanding for staff as they had to wash and dress her, or she would take hours to manage by herself.

When observations at different times of the day were recorded it was noted that:

- When left to cope alone Mrs Black did not seem to be clumsy all the time, for example she picked up a magazine and turned the pages without any problem and when a cup of tea was placed beside her, she drank it in a normal way.
- At mealtimes staff would feed her without allowing her to try to help. Problems intensified when staff said 'Open your mouth, Mrs Brown' or told her to pick up something.
- When dressing or undressing the supervising staff member usually completed the task. Invariably requests to 'Lift your arm' or 'Put Your foot through here' were met with chaos, screams and a push.

After the observations, arrangements were made to keep Mrs Black up at night until everyone else was in bed. She was escorted through to her bed without any request to perform any task. The conversation consisted of comments such as 'It is awfully quiet now, everyone must have gone to sleep' and 'I do like your nightie, it is such a pretty colour'. Within minutes she had undressed herself and was snuggled into bed.

The implications of an apraxia were explained to the staff and all members of staff were encouraged to avoid directing Mrs Black's attention to a task. Distracting her attention was stressed. The reason for her screams and pushing was due to her frustration and her inability to help no matter how hard she tried. An immediate improvement in self care was the result. It required a careful step-by-step programme to fade out the effects of institutionalization and dependency, but when staff realized that it was within Mrs Black's capability to perform movements naturally and automatically, she was given much more opportunity and encouragement to manage by herself.

Case 3 could be confused with Case 1 and it is only by careful observation and enquiry that the real nature of a problem can be clarified.

REFERENCES

Ellis, A.N. and Young, A.W. (1988) *Human Neuropsychology,* Laurence Erlbaum Associates, Hillsdale, NY.

Heilman, K.M., Valenstein, E. and Watson, R.T. (1985) The neglect syndrome, in *Handbook of Clinical Neurology,* eds P.J. Vinken, G.W. Bruyn and H.L. Klawan, Elsevier, Amsterdam.

Kitwood, T. (1990) Dialectics of dementia: with particular reference to Alzheimer's Disease. *Ageing and Society,* **10**, 177–96.

Murdoch, B. (1990) *Acquired Speech and Language Disorders,* Chapman & Hall, London.

Thompson, I.M. (1988) Communication changes in normal and abnormal ageing, in *Neuropsychology and Ageing* (ed. Holden U.P.), Croom Helm, London.

Walsh, K. (1994) *Neuropsychology,* 3rd edn, Churchill Livingstone, Edinburgh and New York.

2

Realistic assessment

There is more than one reason for failing a test ... the way that it is failed is frequently more important than the score.

Ratcliffe, 1987

COMMON PRACTICE

Over the years elderly people have been presented with many forms of test and assessment, very rarely have any of these procedures been of any relevance to their problems, appropriate to their abilities or capable of reflecting their interests and needs. They have suffered from the popular myth that age and intellectual deterioration go hand in hand. Modern research has, at last, discerned the deficiencies in the early work which introduced the dubious concept of the IQ into the international vocabulary. The original constructors of such tests failed to consider a number of variables including the existence of a different cultural society 50 or more years before them. The present 80 and 90 year olds grew up in the Edwardian era and during the First World War, a very different world from the 1930s when most IQ tests were first developed. People grew up with different health, nutritional, educational and environmental systems and opportunities. The tests made direct comparisons between older and younger subjects providing a patronizing extra points allowance for the ageing process. By failing to recognize the variables the early researchers introduced tools reinforcing the myth of natural deterioration which, despite present day findings to the contrary, is proving hard to eradicate.

Currently, certain test batteries continue to be widely used, and the belief that the results are valid remains a common one. Battery-type investigations are often used in large scale projects involving subjects from the community as well as institutions. The Wechsler Adult Intelligence Scale is still applied, and this, or whatever battery is in vogue in a particular area, can be employed indiscriminantly regardless of individual differences or special difficulties. Such an assembly line process is unlikely to supply a meaningful picture of a group, let alone an individual.

Some of the basic errors with this approach are:

- The feelings of the participants are ignored.
- The nature of most tests is inappropriate.
- The questions employed are irrelevant.
- Stress is introduced to an unacceptable level.
- The participants have little comprehension of the purpose of the tests.
- Comparisons between previous and present ability is rarely sought.
- The real priorities of elderly people are omitted.
- There are numerous other omissions, e.g. environmental, neuropsychological, etc.

Batteries are for hens not for people, and even then they are unnatural! They are impersonal, usually irrelevant, stressful and an invasion of dignity and privacy (Holden, 1984).

If a client is threatened by a task or fears that he or she could be shamed by incorrect responses, it is natural to become defensive. The concern to preserve some dignity and self esteem can produce reactions of anger, resentment, embarrassment and even depression. Under such conditions the responses can hardly be seen as valid. It is incredible that assessors are unable to appreciate the implications of the many responses that are common to these investigations. A fragile subject will invariably respond with one or the other of the following comments:

'Would you like a cup of tea, dear?'
'Excuse me, I must go to the toilet.'
'I'm sorry, I haven't brought my glasses with me.'
'I think you had better ask my daughter about that, she would know.'

Most test material has been designed by young people with a younger age group in mind. Many questions and problems are totally inappropriate for older people – Woods and Britton (1985) point out, for instance, that it is rather unusual to discover an 87 year old who wants to find her way out of a forest (Wechsler Adult Intelligence Scale), why is she there in the first place! Equally the abilities required by a forceful young executive, 'Yuppy' or otherwise, are hardly of the same importance to a retired gentleman in his nineties who is more concerned about heating his home and keeping himself healthy than in developing business or in solving world trade problems. Priorities **do** change, though basic interests may not.

The myths surrounding intellectual ability and ageing have been unmasked by researchers such as Rabbitt (1988, 1990) and Schaie and his colleagues (1968, 1990). Research is demonstrating that intelligent young people will probably become intelligent old ones as a vast number of elderly superpersons have been overlooked in the concern over those showing deterioration in social and cognitive functioning. It is important to appreciate that there are people more intelligent than ourselves, that quite a number of them are in care for one reason or another, and that this group will find it extremely exasperating to be treated as intellectually inferior to their supporters.

To place pressure on clients will undoubtedly produce invalid responses. Particularly in large scale investigations the subjects will be puzzled by the purpose of the tasks before them. More assertive people of any age will demand a full explanation and may refuse to co-operate, but many older people will accept a brief outline and could well be totally unsure of the real reason for the exercise. They might feel obliged to co-operate because the interviewer is 'so nice and kind'. The response will probably be what the older person thinks the younger one wants to hear!

It is far more important to obtain a comparison between a person's past and present performance than it is to compare an old and young age group. In research there can be good reasons to find out such differences, but on an individual basis, what is the purpose of looking for differences between the abilities of the person and those of younger, more active people? What **is** important are the differences that have developed in the person's lifestyle, interests and abilities over the years. Rarely are batteries or tests used to examine these important and relevant factors. Information about intellectual level and skilled performance may be desirable, but how can these be evaluated without knowledge of the person's emotional, environmental, physical and neuropsychological status? It is of vital importance to be able to assess a problem in the light of such information. A variety of influences can account for the apparent deterioration of an individual. If these are identified effort should be made to modify them, for they are an essential part of a full investigation where to omit any relevant information, including the possibility of specific brain function changes, will lead to errors in interpretation, management, treatment and rehabilitation, and thus to failure.

There has been considerable research in recent years on how the ageing process affects a person's performance (Rabbitt, 1990; Stuart-Hamilton, 1991). Once this was merely an academic exercise, but now it has real practical implications. Apart from other aspects, sensory changes can result in misinterpretations – a person may not see or hear something clearly and respond incorrectly, so giving a false impression of his or her ability.

Whilst encouraging a more delicate approach to the problem of assessment, it is still important to maintain a collection of relevant test material in a department, so that there is a choice of procedure to meet the needs of each individual client. There are a number of useful accounts and reviews of test materials available which can be consulted (Woods and Britton, 1985; Birren and Schaie, 1990; Stokes, 1992). Although more general methods of evaluating intellectual level and personality are not considered appropriate, there is common ground with any type of investigation which seeks a baseline of ability on which to build, and which provides a suitable setting and environment in which to carry out any necessary investigations.

REASONS FOR ASSESSING ELDERLY PEOPLE

These are probably identical to those for assessing any other age group:

- To obtain a baseline assessment of function – both what can and cannot be done – in order to avoid setting unrealistic goals.
- To monitor change.
- To demonstrate positive changes to the client and to have convincing evidence for those who need to know, e.g. staff and relatives.
- For selection purposes – to ensure that people of similar levels are chosen for either a group or research purposes.
- Research projects.
- To evaluate a new approach, treatment programme, service, etc.
- To assist diagnosis and prognosis.
- For legal purposes, e.g. a head injury.

Routine assessments on admission to hospital or home are not acceptable for that reason alone, nor are routine administrations of a given test acceptable – an individual's needs are paramount.

Preparation for assessment

All staff working with elderly people should begin by learning something about normal older people. The moment a problem appears on the horizon 'abnormality' becomes the priority. Normal older people are, surprisingly, normal! The world is full of remarkable over 70s, or over 80s for that matter, but somehow such independence is overlooked despite the statistics which show that a good percentage of those even over 80 years manage their own life satisfactorily and that only a very small percentage of the 65–70 year group require help.

The need to look more carefully at some of the apparent dependencies has also been emphasized. Kitwood and Bredin (1992) have developed a dementia care mapping programme which is meant to assist in establishing the influences of the environment, as well as people, on patients who could be responding to external influences rather than demonstrating a true cognitive deterioration. As discussed earlier, such negative influences can assist in misleading observers of people in their own homes and result in incorrect 'diagnoses'.

The first step must always be to obtain information about the person's background and history. As this can verge on an invasion of privacy, care and time will be necessary. A team with a social worker member will be an advantage, but there are other questions which will require an answer from other team members. Difficulties arise when the person is confused or unwell. There may be no surviving family member to assist, long time friends may have died or moved away and the neighbours may know very little. The social worker can pick up clues from the home – photographs, the house and possessions, books, various souvenirs – all these have played a role in life experiences. Usually relatives or the person him or herself can fill in details and neighbours might know about routines, likes, dislikes and some of the habits and interests. Even a forgetful, vague, very old patient will provide many indications of previous standards. Previous occupations, travel, skills and interests as well as the occupations and interpersonal relationships of relatives can aid in building up a picture of the whole person.

When an assessment is to be instigated, its aims should be established and also the circumstances in which it will be carried out. Where is it to be held? What is the stated problem, what is already known about the person and who is to carry out the investigation?

In early years those applying test procedures arrived at the interview carrying a case full of test materials. Today it is deemed more appropriate to sit down and simply talk. Establishing a good rapport is vital, without a relaxed and sociable atmosphere the testee will not be able to co-operate properly. If the interview is held in a hospital or home the person is only too aware that this is a strange environment, not his or her **real** home and so can become disoriented or threatened. A patient requires a feeling of ease and reasonable control over a situation before he or she can respond to enquiries which appear to be an invasion of privacy or liable to invoke feelings of embarrassment. An experienced and empathetic clinician or therapist will take time to allow the person to maintain dignity and to be able to answer without pressure. All investigators should be aware of this. If it proves necessary to abandon all ideas of introducing test procedures until another time, or even completely, then the interviewer should have the skills necessary to do so and to be able to use other measures to find the required answers.

To be able to evaluate the significance of any responses to test procedures it is important to know if there is any discrepancy between present functioning and that which was operative before illness developed. This can prove difficult as for many reasons a person may not have had the opportunity to use basic abilities, or to develop skills. Furthermore with highly intelligent people it is often very difficult to detect loss as they can perform impressively; at the other end of the scale it can prove too easy to assume loss though minor cognitive ability has always been present.

Without some baseline indication of ability it is very hard to evaluate performance on tasks, or to set realistic and appropriate goals. If the person is capable of completing a formal test and when a good rapport has been established, the National Adult Reading Test (NART) developed by Nelson and Willison (1983) could prove valuable. Any language difficulty will exclude its use, but in general it does give a good indication of a person's previous educational level. It has recently been reprinted with larger type so that it seems to be more of an eyesight test than a threatening vocabulary or reading test! The more able can also respond with interest to the Block Design Test or to Raven's Coloured Matrices. With the more frail or confused the latter two should be avoided. Of major importance is the identification of strengths as well as weaknesses. Activities of daily living (ADL) should be checked also, once medical examinations are completed. Ideally information from all professionals in a team should be obtained before any conclusions regarding diagnosis or goal setting are made. Such information is relevant to the process of rehabilitation, management or treatment and it is a matter of concern that such teams should be maintained in the community care system. However, even when a good assessment is instigated, there is often an omission in providing good standards of practice as brain function is rarely included. It is unfortunate that staff overlook this aspect and fail to consider the implications of behaviour and ability in this light. To omit neuropsychological factors can result in setting impossible and meaningless goals.

NEUROPSYCHOLOGICAL INVESTIGATIONS

Batteries

Although the use of most battery testing has been criticised as inappropriate, there are, of course, collections of tests for specific functions which, unfortunately, continue to employ the term. These include:

- the Halstead-Reitan;
- the Golden-Nebraska;
- Wechsler's Adult Intelligence Scale;
- Luria's neuropsychological investigation (Christensen, 1975);
- the CAMCOG of the CAMDEX (Roth *et al.*, 1986);
- several computerized neuropsychological investigations have now been compiled (Owens in Burns, 1993; CANTAB, Robbins T.W. *et al.*, 1988);
- AGECAT (Copeland and Dewey, 1991).

There are several collections of tests for specific functions which have proved valuable aids:

- Boston Diagnostic Aphasia Examination (Goodglass and Kaplan, 1972);
- the Rivermead Behavioural Memory Test (Wilson, Cockburn and Baddeley, 1985);

- the Visual Object and Space Perception Battery (Warrington and James)
- and the Severe Impairment Battery (SIB), (Saxton *et al.*, 1993), a new battery still to be extensively tried in practice.

Wilson is also developing a visual neglect assessment.

The use of the Wechsler Adult Intelligence Test, in view of all the more specially developed investigations, would now seem a redundant pursuit. Therapists have persisted in its use as a neuropsychological tool for far too long, despite the continuing protests and objections over the years (Albert 1981; Satz and Fletcher 1981; Woods and Britton 1985; Stokes 1992).

The merits and demerits of the Halstead-Reitan battery have also led to much discussion, but its length, type of sub-test and the practice of using technicians to operate it make it inappropriate for elderly clients anyway. It would be easy to become embroiled in the Golden-Nebraska controversy (Spiers, 1981), but as this battery is also inappropriate its questionable use of the Luria material will be avoided.

Most of the recent introductions listed above do have norms for older adults. The CAMCOG section of the CAMDEX is of value, particularly as a little bit more than a screening test. It is also quite easy to administer to rather confused and fragile clients. The SIB requires only 20 minutes to administer and is designed to pick up specific behavioural and cognitive deficits in those who are severely demented. This is a breakthrough in assessments, but at this early stage its full potential cannot yet be estimated. It promises to be a particularly useful tool, but it may not prove of much value in clarifying the impairents in some of the recently identified conditions causing a dementia.

Computerized tests are not available to all and it is still of great importance to actually work **with** a patient, watching and listening to the responses and not always seeking scores, but a person's ability to succeed. It is also of importance to use empathy and understanding with each client, knowing when to stop, change the subject or make a reassuring comment. Anne-Lise Christensen's version of Luria's work remains a major contribution to neuropsychological investigations and is easily adapted for elderly people. Even here a long demanding series of tests can prove pressurizing, but then Luria himself would not have used the entire procedure, only wishing to find the clues to tell him what it was necessary to know.

A careful selection of items from different sections provides a valuable aid to assessing most of the older people who are capable of coping with a simple test situation. It is even possible to use many of the items at a bedside, or without any forms in view. A study by Blackburn and Tyrer (1985) successively distinguished between Alzheimer's disease, Korsakov's psychosis and control subjects. They used a shortened version of the Luria which included tasks from all sections. It is interesting to note that the subjects attempted almost all the tests.

It was Luria's belief in the need to observe and use common sense which should be the guide in assessing the majority of older clients. The most important question in examining for brain function and ability is 'Can the person do this or can he or she not do it?'. It is not a question of how fast, how deftly or how does this person of over 70 years compare in performance with someone of 20 or so years. It is the responsibility of a neuropsychologist to have available a collection of tests rather than a battery, and to be able to select those that are relevant to further enquiry after a screening process has been completed. Most major procedures do not always provide a clear picture of a given impairment. It may seem suspicious, there may only be minor errors, but such findings should be pursued by other means in order to ascertain that either there is a problem or that for some reason the error was of no significance. Other tests should be administered later and should also be non-threatening.

The more independent older person will respond well to more demanding situations, if the purpose is sensitively and properly explained. However, major problems can arise when working with fragile, very confused or unresponsive clients. It is here that the clinician's imagination, observational abilities and experience become important. Where the investigator lacks an appreciation of neuropsychological factors and has limited knowledge of particular behaviours, he or she is more prone to frustration, annoyance and impatience. Under these circumstances the client can be reported as 'untestable, obviously very deteriorated'. What **is** obvious here is the lack of experience and ability of the investigator.

Some form of mental reminder is often necessary in order to remember what abilities require assessment. Something akin to Figure 2.1 can prove useful. It is very easy to forget to examine one or more functions and therefore obtain an incomplete picture for an initial examination. It is almost always necessary to see a person more than once, but it is helpful to have as much information as possible when an actual assessment, even screening, takes place. After this it is possible to examine the findings for suspicious areas and re-examine those in the light of the non-impaired functions and abilities identified in the initial screening.

Practical or basic neuropsychological investigations

In Chapter 1 definitions were offered for most of the terms used to describe what are called the 'soft signs' of neurology and neuropsychology.

Ideally, for a thorough investigation, the help of a neuropsychologist should be sought. As such an individual is a rare presence in most units staff should be equipped with some basic knowledge and be capable of

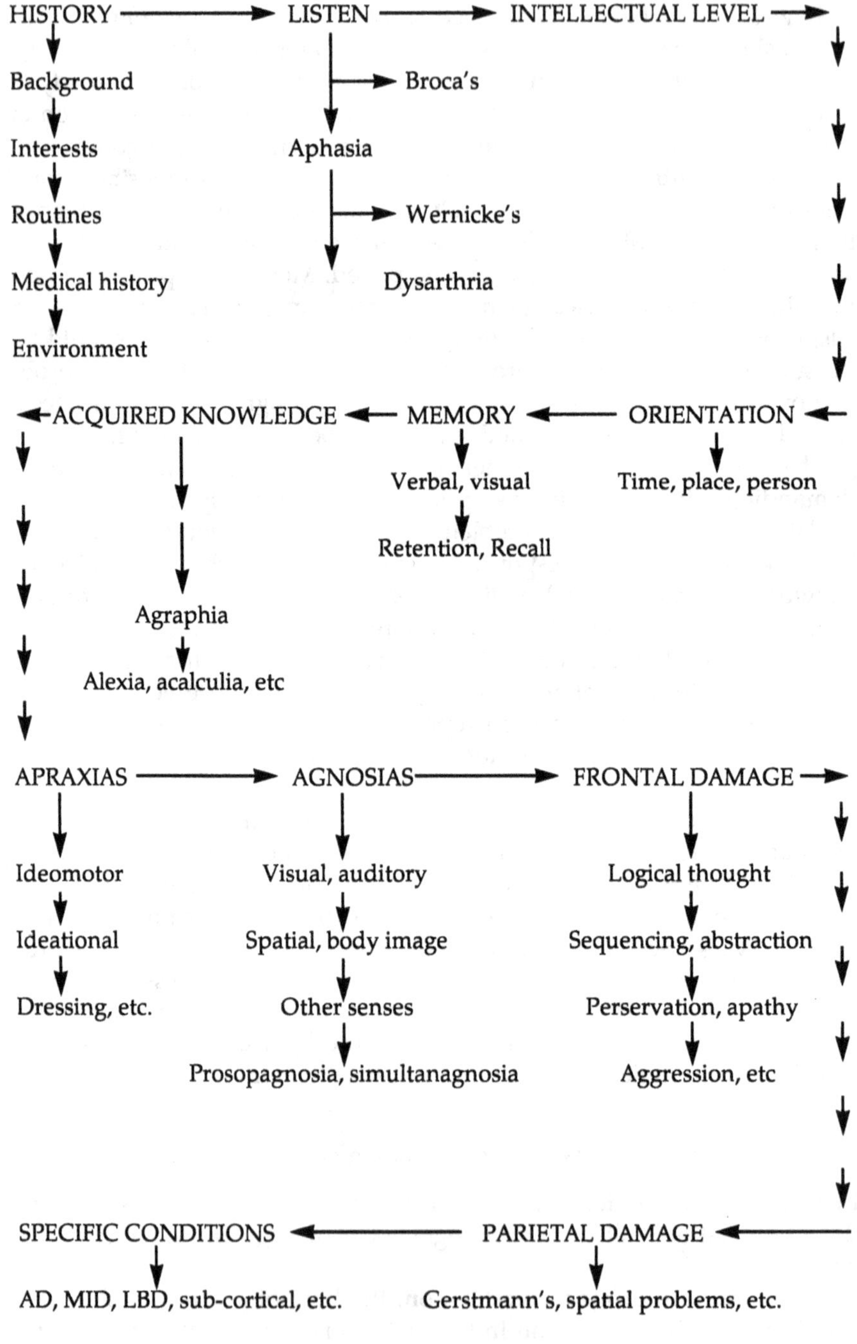

Figure 2.1 Looking for signs.

noting specific impairents. There are simple screening methods which can be employed, and there is always observation. Common sense remains a valuable, though rarely used, approach; with some additonal skill and awareness most staff can find an explanation for their 'instinctive' feelings about a client. Not all situations call for an in depth assessment.

If a patient is very lucid, fluent and obviously capable of managing his or her own affairs and life, it is highly unlikely that aid, other than that of a medical nature, will be required. A person who reads and understands a newspaper, directional signs, forms and letters with ease will not require lengthy investigations of reading ability. If a person has forgotten to bring along reading glasses it is rather stupid to conclude that this is a case of dyslexia!

A person who is capable of all daily living tasks, finds his or her way around without difficulty and recognizes familiar faces is unlikely to have agnosic or apraxic problems of any serious nature. Though it might appear obvious, it is surprising how often lack of required hearing aids, false teeth or glasses lead the observer to remarkable conclusions!

Laterality is another obvious but overlooked clue. With older people in particular it is advisable to establish early in the investigation whether they are right or left handed. Many older people in youth were forced to use their right hand in school instead of the preferred left hand – usually because it was regarded as more socially acceptable. To omit a check on this can lead to misinterpretation and misunderstanding of behaviour and responses. Diagnostic error can result from assuming that a person is a genuine right-hander despite the fact that there is no language disturbance though there is a left-sided paralysis. The real impairments with space and perception are missed and a vascular accident in a person who may be right hemisphere dominant could be overlooked.

An examination setting should give consideration to the following:

- The atmosphere during investigations should be as relaxed as possible.
- The tasks should be geared to the individual.
- The interests, social skills, experience and personal standards gleaned from initial enquiries should be used as far as possible.
- The situation should be friendly, warm and encouraging without being intrusive.
- The aim should be to give the person the opportunity to succeed as much as possible without nullifying the test response.
- The interview should be short. A little at a time is better than too much at once.
- It is better to talk at the first meeting than to push too hard and lose the person's confidence.
- The investigation should be geared to finding the person's retained abilities as well as the impaired or lost ones.

Attention, concentration and comprehension are other factors that should be noted.

As with any other specialty, neuropsychologists each have their own particular area of interest and with overall assessments will place emphasis on certain functions. Albert (1981) for instance stressed: attention, language, memory, visuo-spatial ability, cognitive flexibility and abstraction. Others have a list of areas or functions (as in Figure 2.1) that they investigate during an interview, or develop a mental picture so that when they have completed the tests they are able to link the responses together logically into a meaningful whole. Most staff untrained in the field of neuropsychology are recommended to use such a list, which contains the major headings and includes simple tests for screening purposes.

As the quotation at the chapter heading implies, it is wise to remember that one failure does not imply genuine damage or an impairment; minor errors require further investigation. Perfectly normal people have particular strengths and weaknesses in ability. For example, there are those who cannot tell left from right, but do not have an impairment of brain function which requires treatment – a little retraining perhaps and other drivers carefully avoiding driving along a road behind them! Some people find their way by road numbers and signs, others by buildings and landmarks, some are practically minded, others cannot even hold a saw, everyone is different, so single errors may be of no significance whatsoever. On the other hand when a specific type of task is regularly failed, the evidence is more convincing. However, even minor errors are worth recording as they serve as a means of checking on a possible developing problem – or may even be a sign of recovery.

Initial meeting

The nature of the initial contact depends on the circumstances and the client's degree of disorder. If the person is at home and fairly independent it is possible to discuss the difficulties experienced or perceived, ask questions about his or her history and even to include a few relevant tests. At the same time the reason for the visit can be explained, and stress can be placed on the need to identify the person's strengths so that these can be employed in finding coping or rehabilitation methods. Generally the patient is in hospital or a residential home, here it is vital to establish a good social relationship. Introductions and explanations – simple ones – are required.

The person should be encouraged to talk about him or herself and about the past as well as the present.

One of the most valuable things doctors are taught during training is their need to stand back initially and use their eyes and ears before doing anything else. All professions should receive the same advice, and later, all of them should be reminded to continue the practice as it can be forgotten so easily.

All care workers have the opportunity to observe. Eyes and ears provide invaluable information without a single question being asked.

Listen

It is certain that any interview will involve something to hear, providing there is no sensory defect. The content of conversation is important, but equally important are **how** the person speaks, what response is made, how words are formed and used, what sentences sound like, and how well the person expresses ideas (Table 2.1).

Table 2.1 What do you hear?

Are speech and conversation normal? What does the person say?

- Dysphasia: anomia, mutism, odd words, funny sentences, jargon, poor response, poor understanding, inability to read aloud.
- Dysarthria: correct language, but peculiar production – gutteral, slurred, very low, shaky.
- Perseveration: repeating words, phrases, ideas.
- Confabulation: apparently making things up in response to questions.
- Hallucinatory or delusionary ideas.
- Agnosias: problems recognizing faces, objects, claiming the other person is speaking a foreign language. Not responding to another person talking at one side of him or her.

Aphasia

Careful attention will distinguish between a language problem and a dysarthria. With the latter, sentence structure and words will be perfectly correct, but there is something amiss with the production of sound which is indistinct in some way. A good example of this is Parkinson speech, or **festination** where a person will speak with a tremor in the voice: 'I-i-i-it's a n-n-n-ni-i-ce d-d-day-ay', not a stammer, but a staccatto which may cease once the conversation is underway.

Anomia is a result of a person being unable to find the right word. They will describe an object instead, e.g. 'It is that longish thing there, you use it to write with, it has ink in it' could be a request for a pen.

Expressive, non-fluent or **Broca's aphasia** is usually easy to detect. The person may not be able to speak at all, say only 'yes' and 'no', or use particular words or phrases repeatedly with different emphasis as though the statement was meaningful. 'I don't know what to say' or 'Five, five, five' are examples of the many variations. Social response phrases can be preserved and can lead others to miss the impairment. Rhythm and prosody (correct emphasis on syllables) can also be preserved and can be used to provide some meaning, or apparent meaning, to the words actually spoken.

Mrs Thompson was only able to state repeatedly 'I don't know what to say, I don't know what to say', but she always managed to put different emphasis on the words. On one occasion she was examined on the medical round and then the group discussed her difficulties together. One said in a loud voice 'Well, it's a waste of time asking her opinion about the situation, so we will have to leave her family to decide if she should go into care'. Mrs Thompson, heard this and said with apparent indignation 'Well, I don't know **what** to say, I don't know **what** to say'. It was so appropriate that everyone burst out laughing to the discomforture of the doctor.

When speech is limited it is comparatively easy to note the difficulty, but sometimes it is not so obvious and careful listening is necessary to detect an anomia, the wrong beginning to a word, mixed up parts of a word or missing parts of a sentence.

Fluent, Receptive or **Wernicke's Aphasia,** this may be missed or misunderstood. The lack of response can be interpreted in many ways and only by listening for inappropriate replies to questions can the deficit be detected. Words, phrases and sentences will be used, but they can prove meaningless or obscure. Frequently the person will be upset or even angry if the listener does not understand the attempts to communicate; the client could be unaware of the problem and feel that the other person is being stupid. The help of a speech therapist is highly desirable at this point.

Alexia To investigate this in a relaxed manner all that is required is a newspaper or journal. Simply ask the person to read from it, ensuring that glasses are in use if necessary. Does the patient read correctly? Watch in order to judge if lines, words or parts of the page are missed. If there are letters or cards available, is the writing of relatives or friends recognized? Are the signs on the ward or in a home read without any difficulty? By conducting this enquiry in a natural manner the person should respond naturally too. 'Can you find your way around the ward yet? Let's see, can you read the sign for the bathroom from here? It looks a bit small to me, can you really read it?'

Using newpapapers or magazines in a similarily chatty manner will soon elicit evidence of an ability or lack of ability to read, even if it is only the large letters. It is important to ascertain if the patient understands the words, so some discussion on the topic will prove helpful. Other 'natural' aids will include personal objects such as a box of talcum powder. A possible question could be 'My mother used to like that powder, I recognize the box, what's it called? Oh yes – can you see – it's written here'. By showing the patient the writing it is inevitable that she will attempt to read the name. In this way further insight can be obtained, not only in relation to reading, but also regarding recognition and, perhaps, memory.

Perseveration can be noted during conversation. The term is applied to the repetition of words, phrases or ideas. A thought can be expressed again and again within a matter of minutes. This is usually associated with frontal damage.

Mr Fleming would happily join in any discussion or conversation. Unfortunately he did not get very far before he would say 'Lance Fleming, Lance Fleming ...' and laugh. Even when it was possible to get him to talk about his favourite subject, tennis, he would block in mid-sentence and say either his name or the word 'tennis' accompanied by a sweeping action from the game. As he was also keen on music he was encouraged to hum a tune; it was necessary to interrupt his name repetition and start him off. After a few bars he would stop and say 'Lance Fleming, Lance Fleming' yet again.

Mutism refers to total lack of speech and is caused by a variety of conditions, many of which are sub-cortical in nature. Slowness of speech and of response is another noteworthy finding and could be related to Parkinson's disease.

Confabulation is another problem that can be highlighted during a conversation. Korsakov patients (and patients with amnesic syndrome associated with thiamine deficiency and often alcoholism) often make up convincing responses to questions which concern the past. The content is frequently mistaken for delusions. One lady when asked where she was (in hospital) replied that the year was 1925 and she was at a picnic, that the woman sitting across from her was her sister and it was a lovely day. She was probably recalling a real picnic with her family at about that time ... who can tell?

Psychiatric disturbances such as hallucinations, delusions and paranoid ideas become obvious during conversations. There are many explanations for these – drug effects, Lewy body disease (Chapter 5) or even the truth! There is always the elderly person who talks about being with her mother and is disbelieved by staff as the mother would be a tremendous age – sometimes mother **is** still alive. There is a 'deluded' lady who, when shown a picture of the Queen, made everyone laugh by saying 'She is very familiar, I think I had tea with her last weekend'. In fact, she had been invited to tea at the Palace the previous weekend!

Agnosias By standing to one side of a person (usually the left side) and talking to him or her, it is possible to establish whether or not the person is reacting normally or ignoring input from that side. If there is no response, try touching and then move to a central position and try again.

If a response only comes when on one side and by standing at a point more or less to the middle of the person's nose it is very possible that a **unilateral neglect** is present. If the person also denies the ownership of one side of his or her body, an arm or leg, then **anosognosia** is a problem.

When a person fails to recognize or respond even to familiar faces – including relatives – then damaged facial recognition (**prosopagnosia**) is the most likely explanation. This deficit is far from uncommon and may well be the only presenting problem or the only complaint causing family concern. It can include failure to recognize the person's own face, either in a mirror or in photographs. One couple had great difficulties as every time the husband saw his own reflection he accused his 75 year old wife of having a lover. Apart from that he had no other problem. Women can also fail to recognize their husbands, though there may be a useful avoidance element present, this is hard to prove! One 70 year old insisted that her husband was her father; she could tell the difference with photographs (usually the most vulnerable in prosopagnosia) but not with fact. In some cases rejection or wishful thinking might be the reason; some psychopathology might be present, but usually there is an organic basis.

One patient asked for advice about the strange man who insisted that he was her husband and had the right to go to bed with her. She was deeply concerned about the moral issues and the impression gained by neighbours. After a pause, she added 'He is gorgeous, you know'. Needless to say the therapist advised her to stop worrying and enjoy the relationship. Her reaction to the 'permission' was one of delight!

Face recognition problems can be elicited not only by failure to recognize family and friends, but also by an inability to identify famous faces in newspapers and magazines – this can be used in assessments as added information on the problem.

Look and watch

Watching and observing how a person behaves, reacts, performs tasks and moves about can provide many clues (Table 2.2).

Table 2.2 Look and Observe

- Hands: Normal movements. Tremor. Paralysis. Clubbing. Tapping. Clumsy. Unco-ordinated. Apraxia. Frontal deficits.
- Face: Normal expression, mobile. Fixed facies. Twitches. Laughing/crying inappropriately. Mouthing. Chewing. Lack of expression. Apathetic. Angry.
- Eyes: Staring. Fixed. Lack ability to scan. Funny movements.
- Walking: Normal movements. Strange gait. Ataxia. Paralysis. Loss of limb. Walking into things. Falling.
- Movements: Co-ordinated. Agile. Appropriate. Slow. Clumsy. Odd.

Any signs of unilateral neglect?

Hands it is remarkable that paralysis due to a stroke can sometimes be overlooked, but it does happen. The presence of a tremor can be due to drug side effects, Parkinson's disease, Huntington's Chorea and other conditions. Arthritis and related disorders can cause a hand to curl up or become extremely stiff. Tapping may be a psychological problem and is seen with some Parkinson patients, though it is also seen with some domineering individuals! Apraxia is often present when a person has difficulties with movements.

Apraxias The gestures used by a patient may be an attempt to communicate. If there is a language deficit it may be the only form of expression possible. Gesture is one way of establishing the presence of an apraxia. By asking the person to pretend to wave, to brush his or her hair, an inability to perform a task on request is highlighted. Watch to see if the person can perform the action without prompting.

Notice what happens when the client is presented with a plate of food and a staff member says 'Pick up your knife and fork and eat your lunch'. Do the hands get mixed up and awkward, is the cutlery dropped, held badly, and are hand movements so clumsy that the staff take over? If the food is presented without instruction, merely accompanied by a casual comment such as 'Lunch looks nice today' will the person cope normally? This impairment of simple gesture could be an **ideomotor apraxia**.

Ideational apraxia is demonstrated by mistakes in the series of actions required to perform a more complicated task. The classical example is to ask a client to strike a match and light a candle. Another possibility is to ask 'Please would you take some of the matches out of this box and put them in this empty one?', or 'Here is some money, would you count out six pennies and put them in this purse please?'. In each case a person with ideational apraxia will mix up the sequences and find it impossible to perform the task in the correct order. The matches will probably be on the floor and the pennies scattered. If the person is not told what to do the task will be performed perfectly correctly. In other words when attention is not focused on the task it is performed automatically.

Constructional apraxia is more common than appreciated. The lady who is a productive knitter suddenly has no idea how to make a purl stitch. The cook mixes up the ingredients – too much, too little or none at all. The experienced car mechanic cannot put the engine back together. Sometimes this condition can be observed, but it is not easy to establish its presence simply by watching daily living skills. One or two failures in performing daily tasks are insufficient evidence. Further simple tests can be supplied by the use of jigsaws, mosaics, the block design test from the Wechsler adult intelligence test, or some drawings. Can the person draw a square, cube or box, a star or a clock face saying 10 to five? Often people without any real deficit cannot draw three-dimensional shapes, so if there is a failure, provide a model to copy, draw the shape for the person.

Those with damage to the dominant hemisphere will benefit from a model, but those with damage to the non-dominant area will become more confused. It adds more spatial organization to cope with than they can manage. When the block design is used (only with less impaired patients) the picture patterns also add to the confusion if right-sided damage is present. Rather than drawing it is helpful to use matches or cocktail sticks to build the star or other shapes.

At this point it is advisable to mention unilateral neglect as it can make an appearance during investigations or observations of apraxia. If a patient does not eat the food on one side of the plate, if drawings are incomplete to one side and if the person does not dress one side of the body or turn to look at something happening on one particular side, then it is reasonable to conclude that there is a neglect in operation. A clock drawing, or that of a house with smoke billowing out of the chimney, can be completed leaving out parts to one side. The type of clock with removable numbers used to teach time can be employed here – does the person put **all** the parts back, or are the numbers to one side (usually the left) omitted?

Dressing apraxia is rarely recognized and misunderstanding of this behaviour is the rule and the patient is perceived as unco-operative or unmotivated. It may be due to an inability to relate the clothes to his or her person, to a figure/ground disturbance – an inability to sort out clothes from the surface on which they are laid – or it could be due to an inability to mentally rotate things in space. Parkinson patients have grave difficulty in getting started with a task or even a thought. Admittedly the person could be making difficulties for everyone, but the chances are high that this is related to some form of brain function impairment. If there are delays in dressing it is advisable to consider all the alternatives.

Agnosias Is it necessary for a person to pick up an object, examine it tactilely, put it to the nose to smell it, or put it into the mouth to taste it, before being able to recognize it? Does the person look around in puzzlement for an object and fail to distinguish it until actually touching it? Does the person spend time identifying parts, the surrounding area and a number of possibilities when trying to work out what an object could be? These manoeuvres strongly suggest an inability to recognize an object by the use of a single sense.

Faces, smells, the feel of things and also words and sounds can all be mysteries if the damaged sense alone is employed. It is easy to distinguish an agnosia from an anomia by introducing the use of another sense when a response is usually quick and correct. There are other explanations, however, and these should be investigated at the same time e.g. language, Balint's syndrome (Chapter 3) visual problems, physical loss of taste and smell, arthritis, etc.

Agraphia may be present if the person has problems with writing correctly. Is the pen or pencil held properly, are the words shaped, spelt or completed correctly? Are there many errors or only a few? One of the first things to notice is a hemiparesis – it will not be possible for a person to write if the writing arm is paralysed! Equally important is to be sure that arthritis, Parkinson's disease, Huntington's Chorea or other physical conditions are not operating. Stiff, clenched or clubbed fingers, or those with a shake, will not produce efficient writing.

Anosognosia and **body image disturbances** Unilateral neglect may be suspected if the person omits reading words to one side of a page, writes leaving gaps to that side and ignores half the food on a plate. Does the person get into bed with someone else because the right bed is in the neglected area? A patient will walk into objects, trip over them and ignore people to the neglected side. He or she may not dress one side of the body, deny ownership of an arm or leg and even complain of being assaulted by an arm or hand that 'is not mine'. Staff and relatives will require careful explanation and reassurance if this should occur. Spatial problems can be observed when a previously capable individual is suddenly unable to find the way, read a map or even find the way to the rooms in the home.

Face, facial expression can be an aid to diagnosis. A fixed facial expression can suggest Parkinson's disease. Staring eyes that cannot look down suggest progressive supranuclear palsy (Chapter 5). This latter patient will dribble food over clothes and walk with small steps, feeling the way in case there is an obstacle. Falls are also common.

Inappropriate tears or laughter suggest frontal deficits or a sub-cortical condition. Closed eyes and lack of any response over a given length of time might imply boredom, sleep, a coma or a wish to be left alone, but this situation could also imply a well developed, untreated Parkinson's disease. Enquire if recent behaviour was agitated, even aggressive, causing concern to relatives and staff. Has the person shown signs of one day being quiet and peaceful and then suddenly turning into a racehorse charging about the unit at great speed and proving hard to calm? This evidence of a late stage of the disease process is becoming very rare as most cases are identified and treated early on, but it can still appear.

Apathy and disinterest are as easy to recognize as elation. All may indicate personality changes, clues to frontal damage, though depression must be ruled out as apart from looking miserable, smiling depression also exists.

Twitches, mouthings, eating peculiar things are possibly related to Alzheimer's disease, but can be due to drug side effects. Inability to scan, fixation of the eyes, and various visual field defects are notable signs of specific conditions (e.g. Balint's syndrome) and require neurological examination.

Movements How does the person move? Patients may not move at all – Parkinson patients can experience grave difficulty in initiating movement and once started can have difficulty in stopping. The tiny shuffling step, or **festination** of movement, is typical of this condition.

Wide base gait, ataxia and a variety of funny walks that would make John Cleese jealous are all matters for careful medical investigation. Those suffering from a sub-cortical condition may move at nothing more than a snail's pace and hand and limb movements, speech gesture and thought are markedly slow.

As stated above, walking into things may be due to visual deficits, forgetfulness, but also to unilateral neglect.

Sounds Hearing may be impaired; there are changes in the auditory sense with age that must be considered too. However, if a person fails to jump when a loud threatening noise is emitted he or she may have **auditory agnosia**. This may be related to words, to non-verbal sounds or both. Those with an agnosia for speech, or word deafness, will complain that everyone is talking 'Double Dutch'. Those with non-verbal sound agnosia will not recognize sounds unless they see from whence they come. So, crossing a road and not seeing a fast approaching car which is blasting its horn could prove fatal. The person is not able to identify the sound that he or she actually hears, without seeing its source.

Memory

There are a considerable number of standard test procedures in common use, but their helpfulness with very confused people is as dubious as the value of any other standard investigation. There are a considerable number of variables that must be taken into account when assessing any functional ability level of a confused person (Miller and Morris, 1993) and it is advisable to keep in mind simple measures which can act as a screening method rather than provide a score. Natural, conversational questions are useful: 'Who come to visit you today?', 'What did you have for dinner?'. Does the person know staff names, know anything about recent national or international events or remember the appropriate national holiday when it occurs? In group sessions how successful is he or she when games which require memory are being played? Memory is not only concerned with recent, long term or remote material, it has many facets and a few simple tests will not tap all of them. For those who are capable of more formal testing the Luria Neuropsychological Investigation (Christensen, 1975) offers some easy to apply tests in the memory section.

Most non-verbal tests are far too demanding for frail people and will not supply any useful information. Simple drawings from memory are helpful, as long as the person does not have a paralysis, tremor or other physical difficulty such as poor sight. The use of touch may be relevant with visual problems.

The CAMDEX, CAPE (Pattie and Gilleard, 1979) and mini-mental status questionnaires may be sufficient in severe cases.

Orientation

Mental status questionnaires that can be disguised in conversation make questioning about days, places and the person (i.e. the self) less threatening. The importance of temporal orientation has been overstressed in examination as many healthy people of all ages forget the actual day without a ready cue (Brotchie, Brennan and Wyke, 1985). Those in hospital or care rarely have a good reason to regard one day as being any different from the next. However, the appreciation of whereabouts, the season and events in the near environment are important. In order to avoid any misunderstandings, it is advisable to check that the person has had every opportunity to be aware of what is happening.

For instance, one man had been brought into hospital unconscious after a fall and when he came around found himself in a room where the window looked out on a wall, there was no clock, no newspaper, no calendar and no one bothered to tell him what had happened to him. It was assumed that he was dementing, until his predicament was discovered and when given some information he responded clearly and sensibly, though unsurprisingly with some asperity regarding his treatment.

Acquired knowledge

This is usually covered while investigating language, particularly reading and writing skills. The CAPE provides some baseline tests. Other simple measures would include asking the person to write, read or calculate:

- The girl has a nice dress.
- Persistence is essential to success.
- If oranges cost 10p how much would six oranges cost?
- If six journals cost 25p each how much change would there be from £2?

More difficult problems can be found in the WAIS, Luria or other intelligence tests. It is worth asking the person to write numbers from dictation, e.g. 46, 267, 9481. In most cases there is no problem; some patients will write the tens and hundreds correctly, but once faced with thousands will become confused and write, e.g. 900040081. This is very common with conditions such as Alzheimer's disease – often quite early on – but educational background can be at fault.

Frontal lobe involvement

Damage to the frontal lobes can result from head injury, strokes, tumours, dementia related states and sub-cortical conditions. With elderly people it is always advisable to check for its presence.

Perseveration – the old lady who upsets everyone by her parrot like repetitions may well have frontal damage. Words, phrases, ideas and actions can all be repeated continually. In many cases the repetition is obvious, but sometimes only drawing and writing tasks can clearly elicit it. For instance when writing a paragraph a word will be repeated again and again. While drawing, the same drawing or part of a drawing will reappear inappropriately elsewhere. When asked to remember a series of words or pictures one or two items will reappear on several occasions. Ask the person to continue the following pattern:

0 + 00 + + 000 + + +

One of the perseverative responses could be:

0 + 00 + 00000000

Similarly

It was a lovely day for the picnic

could become:

It wwas a lovvelly day fffor pcicpicnnipic

The stuck needle syndrome occurs when a person is asked to respond to a question or expected to converse normally. Suddenly he or she will get stuck with a topic and will be unable to move away from it. No matter what others say, the thought cannot shift and the person continues to talk about the event, or whatever subject caused the blockage, even a phrase, just like a sticking gramophone needle that has to be moved before the record can continue to play correctly. The responses can sound like fluent aphasia and are often mistaken for this. Some noise, movement or other distraction will intervene, and for a time the person joins in the conversation normally. In due course the needle sticks again and repetition commences once more. Another form of stuck needle syndrome is the inability to change set. When asked to sort things into groups, e.g. coloured shapes, the person can put them into one kind of group, but will find it impossible to progress to another form of group. Either the colour or the shape will be chosen, and then further selection will prove to be a simple variation of the initial choice.

Sequencing problems are seen when a person has difficulty in performing actions in the correct order. Many of the Luria sub-tests are useful in identifying this. Motor sequencing can be tested by asking the patient to perform the following actions, after first demonstrating them:

- With one hand clenched in a fist and the other open and flat on a knee or table, the open and closed positions are alternated simultaneously, as quickly as possible.
- Touching each finger against the thumb, the person counts one, two, three, four at the same time and fairly quickly. After repeating this a number of times the same actions are performed with the other hand.
- Saying and performing the actions – fist, edge, palm – where both hands are made into a fist, then the open hands touch the table with the edge of the hands (palms facing inwards) and finally the palms are placed flat against the table. This is repeated a number of times and should speed up with practice.

Other forms of sequencing which verge on logical thought can be examined by the use of a series of pictures concerning day to day activities – making a sandwich, telephoning a friend, the seasons, the development of a plant. Most occupational therapy departments have some relevant pictures of daily living tasks which are ideal for testing sequencing. Cartoons cut out from newspapers can also be used if each picture is separated, the series presented in a mixed up order and the person asked to put them in the correct order and explain the story.

Abstract thought can show serious deficits as a result of frontal lobe damage. It becomes difficult to see more than the concrete meaning of such sayings as 'A rolling stone gathers no moss'. The response could be: 'Well if it keeps rolling how can you expect the moss to grow, it gets worn off'. The more subtle changes that can occur with abstract thought can explain many observed and often resented behaviours. The person can no longer evaluate his or her performance and behaviour. We will all experience the wish that we did not do this or that, or feel that what we did was good in some way; frontal damage can affect this self evaluation and lack of insight causes the person to show little evidence of concern to behave in an acceptable manner. Sadly this inability to monitor behaviour extends to other people – where most people would be aware that another person did not like or did like something that was said or done, a person with frontal damage may remain totally unaware of others' feelings and needs. This disability can explain why a patient often cannot comprehend explanations.

Logical thought can also be tapped by some of the Luria cards. For instance there are several picture stories that require an appreciation of hidden implications. One cartoon shows an instructor informing the parachutist that he should land on a big, black circle. Unfortunately there is a coal hole of similar dimensions which is mistaken for the landing pad and the unfortunate parachutist makes the wrong choice and falls into the hole. The patient may understand the landing, but may not see the connection between the two dark circles.

Other areas of function which may also be damaged include impaired judgement, reasoning and planning as well as personality changes and the inability to get to the point in discussion or explanation.

Gerstmann syndrome

This is a most controversial topic. Many authorities deny its existence, and yet if all of the suggested signs are present, left parietal damage is probably involved. The signs are: agraphia, acalculia, right/left disorientation and finger agnosia.

Right/left disorientation is simply tested by asking the person 'On what side of you is ...?' and 'On what side of me is ...?'

Finger agnosia can be investigated in several ways, the commonest being as follows:

- The person's hands are flat on the table (or knees) and the examiner presses one finger and asks 'Show me that finger on the other hand'. Then the person is tested through several fingers, but with his or her eyes closed.
- Two fingers are pressed and the person is asked 'How many fingers are there between this one and that one?'. Then the person is tested with his or her eyes closed.

Many people without a particular functional difficulty may make mistakes here. It is the number and type of error that matter – apparent clumsiness, not noticing which finger is touched, stating that there are more fingers between than it is possible to have, etc.

Further comments

Neuropsychological investigations require time and care in order to interpret the results correctly. Neuropsychologists use a variety of tests for specific purposes which may vary from unit to unit. However, when working with elderly people who are frail – both physically and mentally – it must be appreciated that their stress factor is much greater and their resilience much less. To use well established procedures such as the Benton Apraxia or the Boston Aphasia tests would prove inappropriate. In many cases it is only possible to screen for impairments using simple methods, short sessions and a sociable atmosphere. The system of listening, watching and talking as outlined above is probably the best way to obtain necessary information. Staff need a notebook, a list of relevant areas of function, a little imagination plus a lot of tactful concern.

Newspapers and magazines have already been suggested as aids to conversation, but they can also aid screening (Holden and Woods, 1988). A selection of magazines, even though many are years out of date, can prove useful as such commonplace material minimizes threat and helps to build a social atmosphere – thumbing through pages, making comments on pictures and script appears to be a natural thing to do. Chatting about the contents gives staff the opportunity to find the most helpful type of page, preferably one on the left side which is a full page coloured picture, or nearly full page, usually an advertisement. The right hand page should be broken up with pictures, drawings, columns of words, large and small print and, if possible, a photograph of a famous person.

This is a typical magazine layout, but it also provides an easy, relaxed way to screen for a variety of problems (Table 2.3). The person can be requested to point to something or turn a page (apraxia), identify people and objects (agnosia), read, comment on prices and events (acquired knowledge and attention). Obviously this is not quantifiable, and not a full and certain way to identify specific damage, but it can help and act as a guide in difficult situations.

Items listed in Table 2.3 may not cover everything, but in a pleasant, short space of time much information can be gleaned painlessly. Findings

Table 2.3 Information to be elicited using a magazine

Dyslexia	Can the person read – even just large print? Does the person understand what is read?
Prosopagnosia	Are famous faces recognized?
Simultanagnosia	Does the person take in the **whole** picture or only recognize and describe parts of it?
Colour agnosia	Are colours recognized? Can colours be matched to, e.g., a similar colour around or on the person?
Neglect of one side	Where does the person start reading – is it from left to right, or nearer the right hand side of the page? Are some letters missed off the beginning of words?
Memory	Can the person talk about things, events, etc., related to the pictures, information or advertisements on the pages? Can the person recall life events that have just occurred, or future arrangements that have been made?
Apraxias	Can he or she point to items, pick up a magazine, turn the pages on request or match objects in the surroundings with those on the pages?
Comprehension	Does he or she understand what the pictures and articles are about?
Attention	Can the person concentrate for a reasonable period of time on the magazine and discussion?
Speech	How clear is the person's speech? Are there any errors or other difficulties in conversation or reading?

could form the basis to further enquiry and a simple, sociable, reading together session will provide an opportunity to gain the trust and confidence of the person without threat or embarrassment.

GOAL SETTING

In any rehabilitation programme planning plays a major role. Patients have a multiplicity of problems and it can prove hard to ascertain priorities. Frequently totally unrealistic goals are set. This is usually due to the professional perceiving difficulties, not discussing the situation with the person or carer and then trying to impose a programme which is meaningless and irrelevant to the person's perception. This is one explanation of a failed intervention and a vast waste of finances and resources. Other failures are the result of false expectations and inaccurate assumptions, some of which are incorrect diagnoses. When these mistakes occur they guarantee that a person will be faced with further experience of personal failure, with yet more blows to self esteem and confidence.

Lack of knowledge can lead observers to expect a person undergoing treatment to regain abilities that were present previous to an illness – sometimes 5 or 10 years ago. Damage to brain function makes such expectations totally unrealistic and any goal must take such damage into account.

However, retained ability must be sought and employed in any relearning or rehabilitation scheme. Goal setting of a positive nature has been well outlined by Barraclough and Fleming (1986). Here it is vital to stress that part of the foundations for rehabilitation strategies is a good and relevant assessment. Such an investigation should include neuropsychological aspects as well as all the other necessary facets.

Goals can be set with the appearance of relevance, but because of lack of understanding or knowledge regarding hidden disabilities or explanations, these goals can be doomed to failure. Other errors occur in organizing unrealistic or vague stages in order to reach the goal. To use a simple example: Mrs Jones has difficulty in speaking.

The staff's goal is that Mrs Jones will speak fluently. This may well fail for several reasons. If Mrs Jones has a dysphasia rather than a sore throat it will be necessary to identify the physical cause and its nature and degree first. An interim aim of a more appropriate kind might assist poor Mrs Jones in finding some way to communicate her needs.

With the same lady unrealistic stages could have been proposed, for example:

(a) Every time Mrs Jones makes a noise we will praise her and provide more attention.

(b) After she makes more and more noises we will only praise her for the use of a word.

(c) We will only give her attention and praise when she uses a sentence.

It is to be hoped that no one would ever consider setting such stages, but anything is possible! The multitude of dangers resulting from such staging are legion. For instance:

- The lady in question was not consulted.
- Reinforcing noise will lead to a very disturbed ward, patients and staff.
- The chance of Mrs Jones ever reaching stage (b) is highly unlikely as the poor soul will probably require some training on how to make sounds, control them and make words from them.
- She may have difficulty in associating words with objects or anything of meaning to her.
- The damage may be mild and normal recovery will occur in time, or so severe that another form of communication is required.

Without a thorough investigation and the involvement of relevant professionals such a plan will undoubtedly lead to more problems than it sought to solve.

Multi-agency or a real team approach will enable all necessary information to be pooled and parallel approaches made available to all involved. When all staff, carers and the patient are conversant with the real problem, goals and methods used to achieve them, then it is possible to monitor progress and modify and adapt as required.

REFERENCES

Albert, M.S. (1981) Geriatric neuropsychology. *Journal of Consulting and Clinical Psychology*, **49**(6), 835–50.

Barraclough, C. and Fleming, I. (1986) *Goal Planning With Elderly People.* Manchester University Press, Manchester.

Birren, J.E. and Schaie, K.W. (eds) (1990) *Handbook of the Psychology of Aging*, 3rd edn, Academic Press, London.

Blackburn, I.M. and Tyrer, G.M.B. (1985) The value of Luria's investigation for the assessment of cognitive dysfunction in Alzheimer-type dementia. *British Journal of Clinical Psychology*, **24**, 171–9.

Brotchie, J., Brennan, J. and Wyke, M. (1985) Temporal orientation in the presenium and old age. *British Journal of Psychiatry*, **147**, 692–5.

Burns, A. (ed.) (1993) *Ageing and Dementia*, Edward Arnold, London.

Christensen, A. (1975) *Luria's Neuropsychological Investigation*, Munksgaard, Denmark.

Copeland, J.R.M. and Dewey, M.E. (1991) Neuropsychological diagnosis (GMS-HAS-AGECAT package). *Psychological Medicine*, **3**(suppl.), 43–9.

Goodglass, H. and Kaplan, E. (1972). *The Assessment of Aphasia and Related Disorders*, Lea & Febiger, Philadelphia.

Holden, U.P. (1984) The case against standard test batteries. *Clinical Gerontologist*, **3**(2), 48–52.

Holden, U.P. and Woods, R.T. (1988) *Reality Orientation: Psychological Approaches to the 'Confused' Elderly*, Churchill Livingstone, Edinburgh.

Kitwood, T. and Bredin, K. (1992) A new approach to the evaluation of dementia care. *Journal of Advances in Health and Nursing Care*, **1**(5), 41–60

Miller, E. and Morris, R. (1993) *The Psychology of Dementia*, Wiley, Chichester.

Nelson, H. and Willison, J. (1993) *National Adult Reading Test*, 2nd edn, NFER Nelson, Windsor.

Owen, A.M. (1993) Computerized assessment of cognitive function in ageing and dementia, in *Ageing and Dementia*, (ed. A. Burns), Edward Arnold, London, pp. 86–102.

Pattie, A. and Gilleard, C. (1979) *Manual of the Clifton Assessment Procedure for the Elderly (CAPE)*, Hodder & Stoughton Educational, Sevenoaks.

Rabbitt, P.M.A. (1988) Social psychology, neuroscience and cognitive psychology need each other (and gerontology needs all three of them). *The Psychologist: Bulletin of the British Psychological Society*, **12**, 500–6.

Rabbitt, P.M.A. (1990) Applied cognitive gerontology: some problems, methodology and data. *Applied Cognitive Psychology*, **4**, 225–46.

Robbins, T.W. *et al.* (1988) *Cambridge Neuropsychological Test Automated Battery (CANTAB)*, Paul Fry Ltd, Waterbeach.

Roth, M., Tym, E., Mountjoy, C.Q., *et al.* (1986) Cambridge mental disorders of the elderly schedule (CAMDEX and CAMCOG). *British Journal of Psychiatry*, **149**, 698–709.

Satz, P. and Fletcher, J.M. (1981) Emergent trends in neuropsychology: an overview. *Journal of Consulting and Clinical Psychology*, **49**(6), 851–65.

Saxton, J., McGonigle, K.L., Wilhert, A.A. and Boller, F. (1993) *Severe Impairment Battery*, Thames Valley Test Company, Bury St Edmonds.

Schaie, K.W. (1990) Late life potential and cohort differences in mental abilities, in *Handbook of the Psychology of Ageing* 3rd edn, (eds J.E. Birren and K.W. Schaie), Academic Press, London.

Schaie, K.W. and Strother, C.R. (1968). A cross-sequential study of age changes in cognitive behaviour. *Psychological Bulletin*, **70**, 671–80.

Spiers, P.A. (1981) Have they come to praise Luria or bury him? The Luria–Nebraska controversy. *Journal of Consulting and Clinical Psychology*, **49**(3), 331–41.

Stokes, G. (1992) *On Being Old*, The Falmer Press, London.

Stuart-Hamilton, I. (1991) *The Psychology of Ageing*, Jessica Kingsley, London.

Warrington, E. and James, M. *Visual Object and Space Perception Battery*, Thames Valley Test Company, Bury St Edmonds.

Wilson, B., Cockburn, J. and Baddeley, A. (1985) *The Rivermead Behavioural Memory Test*, Thames Valley Test Company, Bury St Edmonds.

Woods, R.T. and Britton, P. (1985). *Clinical Psychology with the Elderly*, Croom Helm, London.

3

Re-examining the concept of dementia

In the past few years research has provided greater insight into a condition which has languished for centuries in the realms of mythology, misunderstanding and misconception. It is supposed that the word 'dementia' was first coined in AD 150 by a physician of Cappadocia called Aretaeus. Presumably he knew what he meant, but over the years there have been so many different definitions applied that the word now inspires confusion and an incredible variety of connotations. By picking up a number of books or articles on the subject it is possible to find that it means, according to different writers: being mad or 'out of one's mind'; global brain damage; certain abnormal brain cells as seen under a microscope; a disorder which causes progressive and irreversible brain damage; brain cell death; a deterioration in social and intellectual behaviour and function, or the usual result of the ageing process. Hardly acceptable as a clearly defined concept!

Invariably dementia has been regarded as a condition in its own right, one that can be diagnosed and one for which there can be no cure or any useful treatment. In the light of recent research it is now possible to recall some of the remarks made in the 1960s by critics of positive attitudes to the treatment of elderly confused people and feel elated by the many proofs which dismiss their pessimism. One such comment on the introduction of positive approaches was 'all they are doing is providing staff with some hope in a situation which is hopeless'. There remain conditions for which there is no answer as yet, but so much has been done to identify reversible conditions, improve management and treatment and to isolate causes and disease processes that the future for those suffering from a condition causing a dementia looks much more promising.

Today the use of the term 'pre-senile dementia' is meaningless; the use of 'senile dementia' implies lack of knowledge or a reluctance to properly investigate a person's problems, and the idea that a living person could be suffering from 'global damage' can only be appropriate if the person is dead or a 'zombie'. The term in vogue at present is 'Alzheimer's disease', mainly because it sounds less pejorative than 'senile dementia', but it too is under careful scrutiny and may well be outmoded in the next 5 or 10 years.

Dementia is **not** a disease in its own right, it is a deterioration in social behaviour and intellectual functioning which presents in a variety of ways according to the condition which causes it and the individual concerned.

Despite a long standing belief that once 'dementia' is present the person will have global brain damage, it is now accepted that 'neurodegenerative diseases do not affect the brain uniformly . . ., psychological processes themselves are regionally organized, and depend on the functioning of specific brain regions' (Neary and Snowden, 1990). In other words, although certain abilities may be impaired as a result of damage to a specific brain area, there are others which are unaffected and which can be employed to assist a person to compensate for loss or adapt to it. Global impairment is possible very late in a disease process and even then who can be certain?

Confusion

Although there are now many safe ways to investigate the reasons behind a change in behaviour and ability, erroneous conclusions continue to be drawn. It is often too easy to assume that because a 68 year old person fails to recognize familiar faces, rambles and behaves strangely that a dementing condition is the cause. A proper examination could reveal a number of explanations – delirium, a variety of physical complaints, shock, anxiety or depression. If a small child behaved in a similar manner a thorough medical investigation would ensue and 'senile dementia' would never be considered.

> Frank Jones was brought into hospital in an unkempt and confused state. It was assumed that he was suffering from Alzheimer's disease. The senior house officer was not satisfied so he carried out a full medical examination and discovered that the patient was suffering from a urinary complaint and required an operation. On further enquiry it was found that the poor man had been so concerned that he might be incontinent in bed that he had not slept properly for several weeks, and had become confused as a result. Once his operation was over and he had slept properly Mr Jones was mentally and physically capable once more.

Post-operative delirium or confusion in elderly people has been a major topic of concern for some years (Lipowski 1989, 1990; Whittaker 1989). In the first century AD Celsus introduced the term **delirium** and it has been recognized throughout the centuries; in 1817 Greiner introduced the concept of 'clouding of consciousness'. However, it is only within recent years that delirium in elderly people has become the focus of research. Frequently it is misdiagnosed or overlooked and thus leads to longer hospitalization, complications and possibly death. Children may have **emergent delirium**, but with older people **interval delirium** may be delayed as long as a week. As staff on surgical wards are unfamiliar with the care of the over 65s, 'senile dementia' can easily be assumed to be the reason for the change in response and behaviour. General surgery in later life is followed by delirium in 10–15% of patients and with certain conditions approaches 50%.

The causes of interval delirium include:

- underlying secondary pathology;
- lack of information and support;
- staff's lack of knowledge regarding care of the elderly;
- too much noise and interference;
- too much or too little light;
- too many changes – faces, bed areas, etc.;
- lack of appropriate sleep;
- isolation.

The effects of interval delirium include:

- mental disturbance can interfere with management;
- sedation may result in more complications and therefore requires great care;
- it has an adverse effect on outcome and may result in a longer stay, permanent damage or death.

It is important that staff:

- assess the patient's functioning carefully and then monitor it;
- investigate any underlying pathology and treat it;
- ensure adequate fluid, nutrition and vitamin intake and maintain electrolyte balance;
- ensure that glasses, teeth, hearing aids, etc. are in use and working as necessary;
- adapt lighting to suit the patient's needs – the sensory environment is important;
- reassure, explain and reorientate;
- watch for pain and the need for the toilet.
- limit noise, unfamiliar faces and places;
- resist waking the patient unnecessarily;
- ensure night staff are aware of needs as they have a major role to play.

A useful rating scale for delirium was developed by Trzepacz, Baker and Greenhouse (1988) which covers the important areas of disturbance: perceptual, hallucinatory, psychomotor, cognition, sleep/wake cycle, etc. It has been criticised by O'Keefe (1994), mainly on the grounds that it does not examine all of the DSM-3 criteria. O'Keefe suggests using the

Delirium Assessment Scale (DAS) introduced by Gottlieb *et al.* (1991), which operationalizes the DSM-3 criteria, although he admits that neither of the tests can satisfactorily distinguish delirium from dementia and that a good history of the onset of symptoms is extremely important.

It is wise to remember that even on geriatric wards or in residential care an elderly person can develop a physical illness and become delirious and may give the impression that a severe dementia has developed.

Dementia at any age

Dementia has always been associated with the ageing population and is often regarded as concomitant with age. Arguments abound on this subject, but there is strong evidence that many very old people die without developing any signs of deterioration – no evidence of abnormal cells or great loss of neurones (Wilcock, 1983). In fact there are large numbers of people over 80 years who continue to be independent, productive, healthy and active.

On the other hand there are many examples of children and young adults who develop a dementia as the result of a number of conditions. Children can have strokes and degenerative, neurological disorders such as Friedreich's Ataxia, Cerebellar Ataxia and an evil thing called sub acute Sclerosing Panencephalitis (SSPE). These are rare diseases, but SSPE is particularly nasty as it frequently leads to death within a short time. An unfortunate child catches the measles, has an apparent recovery, but the virus goes into the blood stream and lies dormant until, usually, about the age of 12 to 13 years. Movements become jerky and involuntary; hallucinations, uncontrollable behaviour, lethargy, intellectual deterioration and epilepsy occur. Improved length of survival and remissions are now possible with recent drug therapy, but so far there is no certain cure.

Progressive Rubella Panencephalitis is clinically similar to SSPE and can lead to death in 2 to 5 years. Alper's disease attacks infants and is transmissible to laboratory animals, causing a spongiform encephalopathy. The use of drugs and glue sniffing are also capable of producing a dementia. There are a number of other conditions which also affect brain function. With children and adults, toxins, poisons and gases can all cause a form of dementia. Various influenza viruses are not particular about age and can result in major life changes for younger people. Strictly speaking, serious head injuries which damage parts of the brain may well result in a dementing condition in later life.

Old age is not the only age vulnerable to degenerative conditions.

Reversible conditions

Usually if an illness, which has dementia as a symptom, can be cured then the dementia should be cured as well. Obviously in some very debilitating situations permanent damage does occur. However, there are an increasing number of conditions where, instead of being progressive and irreversible, dementia can be reversed (Byrne, 1987). Amongst these conditions are:

- pseudo-dementia, including depression;
- effects of drugs and toxins;
- normal pressure hydrocephalus;
- cerebral tumours;
- chronic subdural haematomas;
- nutritional disorders – vitamin B, folic acid deficiency, etc.;
- endocrine disorders – hypo- and hyperparathyroidism, hypopituitarism, etc.;
- neurosyphilis;
- alcoholism;
- other neurological complaints.

In the light of present research it is probable that other conditions will also respond to specific forms of treatment, hopefully including more resistent ones. More detailed accounts of reversible conditions can be found in text by Katona (1989) and Cummings and Benson (1992).

The major problem for the caring professions has been society's tendency to see all older people, particularly those with confusion and odd behaviour, as a homogeneous group and any illness which arises has been labelled with one term so that it has proved exceedingly difficult to select an appropriate form of treatment or management. As this pejorative attitude is being dispelled, more actual conditions are being identified and doors to improved care are being opened.

A NEW APPROACH TO THE CONCEPT OF DEMENTIA

As it has become accepted to view dementia in the light of the condition or disease process causing it, consideration must be given as to how to classify it in a meaningful manner. Until recently the only terms that held meaning for most staff were Alzheimer's disease (AD), Multi-Infarct Dementia (MID) and, possibly, Subcortical Dementia which included Parkinson's disease and Huntington's Chorea. It is now necessary to clarify the picture and to help staff, carers and patients comprehend the new findings in order to use relevant information in practice.

As so many new causes for dementia have been identified, or are in the process of being clarified, most of the epidemiological work is now questionable. Just as dubious are the many studies on dementia where the subjects have been selected on the basis of criteria which can no longer be regarded as reliable (Burns, 1992, 1993). Furthermore the standard diagnostic criteria provided by either the Diagnostic and Statistical Manual of

Mental Disorders (DMS 111R) or the International Classification of Diseases (ICD 10) are now out of date and conditions such as frontal lobe dementia cannot be identified using such guidelines. The new DSMIV has not yet appeared while this book is being written. It will probably not include the more recently identified conditions either.

Neary and Snowden (1990) proposed a useful method by limiting the conditions to those that are associated with progressive degenerative atrophy and transmissible disease and leaving out disorders due to trauma, cerebral vascular disease, hydrocephalus, neoplasia, alcohol abuse and systemic metabolic disorders. As vascular disorders occur in both cortical and sub-cortical areas in a fairly distinct manner they will be included under the cortical and subcortical states in this account:

- Cortical encephalopathies – cognitive changes are most notable.
- Sub-cortical encephalopathies – neurological and physical signs predominate.
- Cortico-sub-cortical encephalopathies – fluctuating cognitive and moderate physical signs.
- Multi-focal encephalopathies – severe cognitive and physical disturbances.

As recent research has identified prion disease more distinctly, multi-focal encephalopathy will be entitled prion disease in the chapter concerned.

Cortical encephalopathies

The main encephalopathies involving the cortical area are Alzheimer's disease (AD), frontal dementia, progressive aphasia and possibly a parieto-occipital disorder called Balint's syndrome.

Frontal dementia

Several of these cortical encephalopathies have not been widely recognized and can be considered 'new' dementia. Frontal dementia is probably the most important of these. Although it is yet to be operationally defined fully there are features which distinguish it from AD (Gustafson, 1987) (Table 3.1).

The initial stages usually show changes in mood and personality, including a bland indifference and then a neglect of self care. The person may become unusually rude without any concern for this behaviour (Orrell, Sahakian and Bergmann 1989). Memory and visuo-spatial skills are preserved until the very late stages. Although frank aphasia does not occur, speech is reduced over time and may result in mutism. Verbal fluency tasks are useful here (Johanson and Hagberg, 1989). The behaviour associated with the frontal lobe syndrome is much in evidence – indifference, outspokenness, lack of attention and perseveration. Elderly

Table 3.1 Frontal lobe dementia (FLD)

Onset 50 to 60 years, insidious, mainly familial (50%), commoner in males.
Makes up 16% of organic dementias (Brun, 1987).
20% primary cortical atrophy.
Atrophy of fronto-temporal cortex.
Loss of large cortical neurones, spongiform changes.
No AD histology.
Very few neurological signs, but syncopal attacks.
EEG normal, CT scan (computerized tomography) shows cerebral atrophy (mainly frontal).
Position emission tomography (PET) shows anterior abnormalities.
Social and personal personality changes.
Unable to manage own affairs.
Irresponsible – loses job, impaired judgement.
Apathy with low motivation **or** over-active, disinhibited.
No insight.
Loss of emotional empathy and social awareness.
Possible stereotyped behaviour – rituals, perseveration, over eating, food fads.
Echolalia and expressive dysfunction – mutism.
Changes in writing, failures on frontal tests.
Praxis and visuospatial skills relatively intact.

patients are particularly prone to self neglect despite preservation of intellect and memory (Orrell and Sahakian, 1991). This picture does not fit the DSM-3-R diagnoses of personality disorder, delirium or major affective syndrome and so the condition can be missed.

Table 3.2 examines the differences between FLD and AD. More detailed accounts of FLD can be obtained in articles by Brun (1987), Gustafson (1987) and Hodgson and Barrett (1993).

Table 3.2 A comparison of frontal lobe dementia (FLD) and Alzheimer's disease (AD)

FLD	AD
Personality changes	No personality change until late
No memory failure	Memory failure
Possibly a temporary dyspraxia	Dyspraxia
Spatial ability spared	Spatial disorientation
No logoclonia (stuttering speech)	Logoclonia
Preserved language function, but eventual mutism	Receptive (Wernicke's) aphasia Paraphasia Jargon
Few neurological signs	Some neurological signs
Normal EEG	Abnormal EEG
No plaques or tangles	Plaques and tangles
Frontal neuropsychological signs	Rarely frontal changes, mainly posterior

Cole (1992) found that 10% of first admissions to a day unit showed an FLD clinical picture. He also pointed out that as many patients may not fulfil the standardized diagnostic criteria for dementia, such patients would be excluded from dementia studies, and as the particular impairments are rarely elicited in a well structured situation such as a medical consultation, FLD can easily be missed. When using neuropsychological tests it is vital to note, not the extent of failure, but the **manner** in which a test is failed. There remain many questions about FLD which are still being investigated. A number of researchers have noted that because of the varying pathologies encountered there may well be several sub-types and differing causes for the condition.

Mary Charles (63 years) has been an active woman, however, her family have become most concerned about the change in her behaviour during the last 12 months. She has begun to repeat what they say and even copy funny gestures that they make accidentally. Food fads have developed and either she refuses to eat once acceptable things, or she gorges herself on anything she can reach. A variety of rituals occur throughout the day – constantly checking doors, counting objects on a shelf, etc. Once a talkative, smiling woman, there is hardly a word or even a smile from her and she walks about stiffly and ponderously, although quite quickly. There seems to be a lack of concern or aloofness about her, although she is pleasant enough in conversation. She knows what is going on around her, finds her way about with ease, appears well orientated and in touch with current events. It is hard to judge if her memory and perceptions are within normal, but from the way she acts they do seem to be intact.

Slowly progressive aphasia

This is another of the newly identified conditions (Table 3.3), distinct from Alzheimer's, which was described by Mesulam (1982). Lobar atrophy occurs in the dominant hemisphere language area.

Several writers have identified adults from a wide age range who have shown no signs of dementia, vascular disease or inability to carry on their affairs and who had no deficits in insight or judgement. However, in each case various language problems have developed and follow-up over 10 years has demonstrated a progressive deterioration in speech, reading and writing, sometimes also in calculation (Chawluk et al., 1986; Kirshner et al., 1987; Goulding et al., 1988).

Table 3.3 Slowly progressive aphasia

Slowly progressive aphasia
Selective atrophy of peri-sylvan region of dominant hemisphere
Probably not genetic
No Alzheimer pathology
EEG normal
CT scan shows atrophy in the dominant hemisphere; PET shows impairment in the dominant hemisphere
There may be no neurological signs; may have right sided tremor, akinesia with mild spastic weakness
Aphasia:
fluency poor or lost
impaired speech production
impaired repetition
anomia
dysgraphia, dyslexia
comprehension impaired
eventual mutism
No other signs of cognitive or behavioural impairment, although depression is often present

Jean Marks, aged 48 years, noticed difficulties in her speech, reading and writing. She worked as a laboratory technician and had a number of hobbies including ballroom dancing, painting and cooking. None of these were affected and she was perfectly capable of coping with her job and daily living. After several years the language problems became so severe that she was referred to a neurologist and was thoroughly investigated. She was forced to leave her job, although no evidence of any cognitive impairments was found other than those related to language. Her spelling was poor, she could not write properly and did not understand written words. A CT scan showed evidence of left hemisphere atrophy. She became increasingly depressed and in the next few years ceased to speak at all.

Balint's syndrome (BS)

Balint's syndrome is fairly rare and the parieto-occipital areas are those primarily affected. However, since it was first identified various reports from a variety of researchers have described patients of all ages with similar problems and a wide range of possible causes. Gunshot wounds, tumours and cerebral vascular accidents are amongst the reported lesions involved (Allison *et al.*, 1969; Verfaellie, Rapcsak and Heilman, 1990).

More recently, BS has been associated with Alzheimer's disease (Mendez *et al.*, 1990; Hof *et al.*, 1990) but, in view of the variety of pathology reported in the literature, it is difficult to accept that AD is the cause or that there is a genuine association.

With BS specific visual association areas are disrupted, though these are normally spared in AD. It is possible that, as in the case of multi-infarct dementia (MID), there is no reason why AD and BS cannot both be present.

BS was first identified by Balint in 1909 who called it 'psychic paralysis of visual fixation'. He identified three types of deficit:

(1) Psychic paralysis of visual fixation is demonstrated by an inability to look towards a point in the patient's peripheral visual field. Ocular mobility is usually normal under automatic control.
(2) Optic ataxia is an inability to execute co-ordinated voluntary movements in response to visual stimuli.
(3) Disturbance of attention. Although attention is normal for non-visual stimuli, it is damaged for visual stimuli.

Another way to describe the syndrome is to say that it is an acquired disturbance resulting in an inability to see what is in the visual field as a whole – a simultanagnosia or something akin to this disorder – in turn this means that the person can only focus on certain areas, becomes fixed on those and cannot shift the gaze at will to another point, nor is he or she able to visually locate an object correctly in order to actually touch it.

When the patient's gaze fixes on some part of the visual field the person will fail to notice or orientate to other things in the periphery. The object or point upon which focus has fixed can move about erratically and it is possible that, by chance, a new stimulus from the periphery will actually fall into the area in focus as the centre of vision shifts. Tests described above for simultanagnosia will help to identify this difficulty. Moving objects can, obviously, cause the person severe difficulties.

Optic ataxia is demonstrated by an inability to reach out and pick up or point to an object. The person can point correctly to his or her own body parts, or to the source of sound, but not towards external objects. Ask the patient to pick up a pencil or a cup of tea and the hands will miss the object by a few centimetres.

As with most apraxias, the patient with optic apraxia cannot voluntarily look correctly at either a new stimulus or respond correctly to a request to look at a particular object or occurrence. This was called 'psychic gaze paralysis' by Balint.

All of these problems must be present for a diagnosis of Balint's syndrome. Recent writers believe that it is due to bilateral damage of the parieto-occipital region and that it is the result of infarctions between the anterior and posterior cerebral arteries. The main cause is probably sudden and severe hypotension and to a lesser extent secondary tumours.

Many elderly people with Balint's syndrome have a vulnerability to systemic blood pressure drop. It can occur after open heart surgery too.

Vascular accidents occurring in the cortex

Multi-infarct dementia (coined by Hachinski *et al.* 1975) is associated with vascular damage in the cortex and sub-cortex – lacunae states and other conditions such as Binswanger's disease are vascular incidents in the sub-cortex which will be discussed in a later section.

Briefly, the usual signs of MID are:

- abrupt onset;
- stepwise changes;
- clear-cut neurological signs and symptoms;
- usually a history of hypertension and previous strokes;
- a fluctuating course – episodes varying in degree of severity and resulting deficit.

MID is a result of a series of strokes of varying degrees of severity with varying gaps of time in between, which progressively lead to extended damage to parts of the brain and associated functions.

There is some controversy regarding the prevalence of MID. Studies suggest it varies between 8 and 30% of people suffering from dementia-related conditions. It can also co-exist with other degenerative states. The condition has been described in detail by many writers including Cummings and Benson (1992) and Katona (1989). Although detail will be avoided here, it is relevant to stress that even if a person has had a stroke, it does not mean that the person is suffering from MID. In addition, although death can result from a severe stroke, many patients recover well and may never have another cerebral accident.

Early diagnosis and treatment are important in order to arrest deterioration and encourage at least some degree of recovery. Patients with MID do not have global impairment, except possibly in very severe cases and at approaching death. In most instances there will be some functional areas intact or only temporarily impaired. Unfortunately it is not always easy to identify the retained abilities, but that should not be a reason to dismiss a person as a hopeless case incapable of doing anything. It is still the concern of the caring profession to try to find retained abilities, use these in rehabilitation or to maintain as much independence as possible and continue to recognize the 'personhood' of the patient.

In 1987 Hachinsky coined another term: **leuko-araiosis** (LA; leuko = white, araiosis = reduced density). LA is used to describe the reduced density of white matter, not previously visible, that was noted on MRI scans. These findings resulted in further studies to examine the implications and nature of LA.

George *et al.* (1986a, 1986b) found no evidence of LA in younger subjects, but an increasing presence with age: 7% in the 55–69 age group and 24% in the 70–85 age group. He stressed that that there did not appear to be a relationship between the severity of a dementia and the amount of LA. However, other studies did not substantiate these findings and some even found that LA in apparently normal individuals could co-exist with disturbances in time orientation, sentence construction and memory. Physical signs can occur too, such as an abnormal gait and reduced limb strength (Prencipe and Marini, 1989).

There is no clear evidence that the presence of LA indicates a dementing condition. However, another study (Coffman *et al.*, 1990), using normal subject (50–60 years) and healthy offspring of probable Alzheimer patients, found that more than half of the offspring had patchy LA, yet the controls had none. LA is prevalent in MID – both cortical and subcortical – but it has been found in Alzheimer's patients too. The fact that LA is present in relatives of Alzheimer's patients does not mean that they will develop the condition too. What it does mean is still to be clarified. However, Ferrer *et al.* (1990) suggest that arteriolosclerotic leucoencephalopathy (ALE) in the elderly (white matter lesions associated with atherosclerosis and arteriosclerosis) is common and is probably the cause of LA, that ALE is asymptomatic and may not be associated with severity of neurological deficits and that dementia in patients with ALE may be caused by degenerative conditions rather than vice versa.

This interesting development will undoubtedly produce further studies and more information about the nature of brain changes with age and the implications of such changes. LA will be discussed further in the section on lacunar states.

Alzheimer's disease

Until recently AD was believed to be responsible for approximately 50% of all cases where dementia was involved. At one time any confusion or cognitive change resulted in a label of 'senile dementia', now AD is in vogue and is probably cited as the diagnosis more frequently than it should be. Homer *et al.* (1988) conducted neuropathological examinations after the death of a number of elderly patients and found that clinical diagnosis during life was not supported by the necropsy findings. In fact 7 out of 13 diagnoses of AD were incorrect. Gottfries (1988) also states that clinical research has not kept in step with neurobiological research and that diagnosis is too simple, particularly in view of the fact that AD cannot be confirmed until after death. He states

> 'it may be of value to divide primary degenerative dementias into sub-groups based on the findings obtained with brain imaging techniques . . . the dementias could be divided into frontal lobe

dementias, parieto-temporal dementias, subcortical dementias and dementias with diffuse degeneration or with no visible degeneration. The AD/SDAT group of dementias could then be referred to the parieto-occipital lobe dementias'.

GOTTFRIES, 1988

Burns (1993) cites the McKhann *et al.* (1984) criteria for the diagnosis of AD as the most consistently accurate available according to a number of studies. Despite these opinions, it is doubtful that they will be capable of discerning the recently identified conditions or differentiating them from AD. Frontal dementia will not be picked up and Lewy body dementia will be misdiagnosed. Byrne, Smith and Arie (1991) concluded that the criteria for diagnosing AD are very variable and the aetiological causes remain unclear. It seems unlikely that the new DSM-IV will prove more discerning.

For some years there have been doubts expressed that AD is a single condition and sub-groups have been suggested. However, when these sub-groups are examined closely it becomes very difficult to accept the relationship at all. For instance, originally Alzheimer described cases of cognitive change in people under the age of 65 years. This led to the use of the term **pre-senile** and a belief in two conditions which were controlled by the gap between 64 and 65 years – a patient of 64 years had pre-senile dementia, but a 65 year old had the senile variety! Later this artifical split was considered unnecessary as there was little evidence to show any difference between signs and symptoms in the young and older age groups. More recent research has found substantial differences and is distinguishing between people developing changes particularly in the parietal lobes and those who are mainly in their late 70s or into their 80s who have temporal lobe changes (Blennow, Wallin and Gottfries, 1991; Han and Birkett, 1993). Other differences are also apparent, to such an extent that it is hard to accept that the disease process is the same. Table 3.4 outlines the problem of differentiating between two varieties of AD. The age factor should not be considered until post 70 or even 80 years.

When examining the comparisons in Table 3.4 it becomes exceedingly difficult to see any logic in referring to the two 'sub-groups' as the same condition. It would seem more appropriate to call EAD parietal dementia and LAD temporal dementia or, perhaps more acceptably, parietal disorder and temporal disorder.

Various studies on risk factors (Amaducci and Lippi, 1992; Baker *et al.*, 1993) have indicated particular risk from severe head injury (Graves *et al.*, 1990a; Roberts *et al.*, 1991) and this possible link is being investigated further. Other risk factors that have been investigated include:

Table 3.4 Alzheimer's disease

EAD = early onset or type 11 AD	LAD = late onset or type 1 AD
Parietal signs	Temporal signs
Many neurofibrillary tangles (NFTs)	Very few NFTs
	Possible vascular factors
No white matter lesions	White matter lesions
Minor central atrophy	Major central atrophy
No sub-cortical signs	Sub-cortical involvement (myoclonus*, rigidity, akinesis†)
Vitamin B12 normal	Diminished B12
Severe cell loss	Minor cell loss
Impairment of language	Language more or less normal
Severe neurotransmitter loss	Minor neurotransmitter loss

* Myoclonous = jerky movements.
† Akinesis = a slowing of movement or a delay in initiating movement of the limb contralateral to a lesion.

- Maternal age at birth – some controversial evidence exists to suggest that increasing parental age may be a possible risk.
- Association with animals – negative findings.
- History of chest pain – negative findings.
- Self reported renal disease or hypertension – negative findings.
- Age – a steep increase in the prevalence and incidence of dementia.
- Sex – in most Western cultures age-adjusted rates for women were higher than for men.
- Relatives – if there are a number of relatives with a dementia, this could be a risk factor, especially in early onset cases.
- Down's syndrome – there is still a question mark about an association, but there is evidence to suggest that a family history of Down's could prove to be a risk.
- Environmental factors – specific types of exposures appear to be risk factors, but these will be discussed in another chapter.

Smoking, surprisingly, has been found in many studies to be a non-risk factor, and, even more surprising, several studies have indicated that the risk of developing AD actually decreased with the number of cigarettes smoked! (Graves *et al.* 1990b; Van Duijn and Hofman, 1991). Although several studies have findings implying nicotine may be anti-AD, in fact one form of therapy uses nicotine as a treatment. The unfortunate smoker is still left with the knowledge that cigarettes are bad for the health in other ways!

Another interesting finding (Dewey, Davidson and Copeland, 1988) should prove to be a cheering thought for those suffering from headache and migraines – apparently several studies have identified a decreased risk of dementia for this group of people!

A further complication in considering AD as a single condition is the presence of **familial AD** or FAD. This probably came into focus as a result of investigations into risk factors, though the literature has described families with a high rate of dementia for many years.

The fear of FAD is a matter of social concern as, on the basis of incomplete research, several articles and books have been published which could give rise to changes in public attitudes. The tragic people suffering from AIDS have been faced with problems including diminished social contact, difficulties in job finding and even in obtaining mortgages. If FAD becomes accepted as a mainly familial disease a similar situation may arise with families, where even one case of AD has been reported. Miner (1989) provides a good overview of the condition and problems, but some of the chapters prove disturbing reading and are full of speculative ideas which could be most disconcerting for families. Genetic counselling is suggested, but in view of the lack of established knowledge about FAD this would seem to be a dangerous avenue for general practice and could only lead to public changes in attitude, not to mention excessive fear for relatives.

AD is not entirely genetic in nature – the case where one identical twin develops AD and the other does not is proof of this. Furthermore it is possible that a person liable to develop AD may die before this occurs. Some studies suggest that 50% of AD is familial, others quote 15%. At this stage of research it is not possible to make a definite statement. There is no doubt that there are families who do demonstrate a large number of relatives suffering from AD, even ethnic groups such as the Volga Germans who seem particularly prone to this disease. However, sporadic AD does appear to be the commonest form – if the condition can actually be termed AD.

It has been easier to examine early onset AD, but it remains difficult to separate the signs of FAD from sporadic AD as the presentation appears to be the same and only a genetic factor can differentiate between them. St George-Hyslop *et al.* (1987) and his team were the first to show a linkage to markers on the long arm of chromosome 21 and begin the search for specific mutations or changes within a gene which would cause AD to develop. The familial link with Down's syndrome and AD has played a role in this research. The picture remains far from clear, though the beta-amyloid precursor protein (APP) gene is under close scrutiny. The amount of work in progress promises to clarify the genetic factors in the near future (Mullan, 1991; Mann, 1993).

Although FAD appears to be similar to what is called early Alzheimer's there is still no evidence to show a similarity with the late onset type. This confusion over EAD, LAD and FAD leads to confusion over treatment and management approaches, as a different strategy is required with each of them. It is also difficult to logically associate these differing states with a single concept and the term Alzheimer's disease becomes meaningless.

For those interested in obtaining a more detailed account of present research on the causes of AD there is a constant flow of articles on various aspects. Wilcock (1988) provides a general account including the relevance of neurotransmitters such as the cholinergic system. Edwardson (1991) discusses the controversial issue of the effects of aluminium and other environmental influences are covered by Calne *et al.* (1986).

REFERENCES

Allison, R.S., Hurwitz, L.J., Graham-White, J. and Wilmot, T.J. (1969) A follow up study of a patient with Balint's Syndrome. *Neuropsychologica*, **7**, 319–33.

Amaducci, L. and Lippi, A. (1992) Risk factors for Alzheimer's Disease. Editorial. *International Journal of Geriatric Psychiatry*, **7**, 383–8.

Baker, F.M., Jordan, B., Barclay, L. and Schoenberg, B.S. (1994) Risk factors for clinically diagnosed Alzheimer's Disease. *International Journal of Geriatric Psychiatry* **8**, 379–85.

Blennow, K., Wallin, A. and Gottfries, C.G. (1991) Presence of parieto-temporal symptomatology distinguishes early and late onset Alzheimer's Disease. *International Journal of Geriatric Psychiatry*, **6**, 147–54.

Brun, A. (1987) Frontal lobe degeneration of non-Alzheimer type. 1. Neuropathology. *Archives of Gerontological Geriatrics*, **6**, 193–208.

Burns, A. (1992) Accuracy of clinical diagnosis of Alzheimer's Disease. *Alzheimer's Review*. Parke-Davis, Magellan Medical Publishing, London.

Burns, A. (ed.) (1993) *Ageing and Dementia*, Edward Arnold, London.

Byrne, E.J. (1987) Reversible dementias. *International Journal of Geriatric Psychiatry* **2**, 73–81.

Byrne, E.J., Smith, C.W. and Arie, A. (1991) The diagnosis of dementia – 1 clinical and pathological criteria: A review. *International Journal of Geriatric Psychiatry*, **6**, 199–208.

Calne, D.B., McGeer, E., Eisen, A. and Spencer, P. (1986) Alzheimer's Disease, Parkinson's Disease and Motorneurone Disease: Abiotropic interaction between ageing and environment. *The Lancet*, 8 November, 1067–70.

Chawluk, J.B., Marsel Mesulam, M., Hurtig, H. *et al.* (1986) Slowly progressive aphasia: Studies with positron emission tomography. *Annals of Neurology*, **19**, 68–74.

Coffman, J.A., Torello, M.W., Bornstein, R.A. *et al.* (1990) Leukoaraiosis in asymptomatic offspring of individuals with Alzheimer's Disease. *Biological Psychiatry*, **27**, 1244.

Cole, A.J. (1992) A survey of Frontal Lobe Dementia in a psychiatric Day Unit population. *International Journal of Geriatric Psychiatry*, **7**, 731–8.

Cummings, J.L. and Benson, D.F. (1992) *Dementia: A Clinical Approach*, Butterworth-Heinemann, Boston.

Dewey, M.E., Davidson, I.A. and Copeland, J.R.M. (1988) Risk factors for dementia: Evidence from the Liverpool study of continuing health in the community. *International Journal of Geriatric Psychiatry*, **3**, 245–9.

Edwardson, J.A. (1991) Alzheimer's Disease and aluminium. *Alzheimer's Review*. Parke-Davis, Magellan Medical Publishing, London.

Ferrer, I., Bella, R., Serrano, M.T., *et al.* (1990) Arteriosclerotic leucoencephalopathy in the elderly and its relation to white matter lesions in Binswanger's Disease, multi-infact encephalopathy and Alzheimer's Disease. *Journal of Neurological Sciences*, **98**, 37–50.

George, A.E., de Leon, M.J., Gentes, C.T.R. *et al.* (1986a) Leukoencephalopathy in normal and pathological ageing 1. CT of brain lucences. *American Journal of*

Neuroraudiology, **7**, 561–6.

George, A.E., de Leon, M.J., Kalnin, A., *et al.* (1986b) Leukoencephalopathy in normal and pathological ageing 11. MRI of brain lucences. *American Journal of Neuroraudiology*, **7**, 567–70.

Gottfries, C.G. (1988) Alzheimer's Disease: A critical review. *Comparative Gerontology C.*, **2**, 47–62.

Gottlieb, G.L., Johnson, J., Wanich. C. and Sullivan, E. (1991) Delirium in the mentally ill: operationalizing the DSM-3 criteria. *International Psychogeriatrics*, **3**, 181–96.

Goulding, P.J., Northern, B., Snowden, J.S., *et al.* (1988) Progressive aphasia with right-sided pyramidal signs: another manifestation of localized cerebral atrophy. *Journal of Neurology, Neurosurgery and Psychiatry*, **52**, 128–30.

Graves, A.B., White, E., Koepsell, T., *et al.* (1990a) The association between head trauma and Alzheimer's Disease. *American Journal of Epidemiology*, **131**(3), 491–501.

Graves, A.B., van Duijn, C.M., Chandra, V., *et al.* (1990b) Alcohol and tobacco consumption as risk factors for Alzheimer's disease. *International Journal of Epidemiology*, **20**(suppl. 2), 558–61.

Gustafson, L. (1987) Frontal Lobe degeneration of non-Alzheimer type. 11. Clinical picture and differential diagnosis. *Archives of Gerontological Geriatrics*, **6**, 209–23.

Hachinski, V.C., Iliff, L.D., Zilhka, E., *et al.* (1975) Cerebral blood flow in dementia. *Archives of Neurology*, **32**, 632–7.

Hachinski, V., Potter, P. and Merskey, H. (1987) Leuokaraiosis. *Archives of Neurology*, **44**, 21–3.

Han, L. and Birkett, D.P. (1993) Alzheimer's Disease in the old and the young. *International Journal of Geriatric Psychiatry*, **8**, 481–6.

Hodgson, R.E. and Barrett, K. (1993) Dementia of frontal lobe type in monozygotic twins. *International Journal of Geriatric Psychiatry*, **8**, 431–4.

Hof, P.R., Bouras, C., Constantinidis, J. and Morrison, J.H. (1990) Selective disconnection of specific visual association pathways in cases of Alzheimer's Disease presenting with Balint's syndrome. *Journal of Neuropathology and Experimental Neurology*, **49**(2), 168–84.

Homer, A.C., Honavar, M., Lantos, P.L., *et al.* (1988) Diagnosing dementia: Do we get it right? *British Medical Journal*, **297**, 894–6.

Johanson, A. and Hagberg, B. (1989) Psychometric characteristis in patients with frontal lobe degeneration of non-Alzheimer type. *Archives of Gerontology and Geriatrics*, **8**, 129–37.

Katona, C.L.E. (ed.) (1989) *Dementia Disorders: Advances and Prospects*, Chapman & Hall, London.

Kirschner, H.S., Tanridag, O., Thurman, L. and Whetsell, W.O. (1987) Progressive aphasis without dementia: two cases with spongiform degeneration. *Annals of Neurology*, **22**, 527–32.

Lipowski, Z.J. (1989) Delirium in the elderly patient. *New England Journal of Medicine*, **320**, 578–82.

Lipowski, Z.J. (1990) *Delirium: Acute Confusional States*, Oxford University Press, New York.

Mann, D.M.A. (1993) The molecular pathology of dementia. *Current Opinion in Psychiatry*, **6**, 549–56.

Mesulam, M.M. (1982) Slowly progressive aphasia without generalized dementia. *Annals of Neurology*, **11** 592–8.

McKhann, G., Drachman, D., Folstein, M., *et al.* (1984) Clinical diagnosis of Alzheimer's Disease: Report of the NINCDS-ADRDA Work group under the auspices of Dept Health & Human Services Task Force on Alzheimer's Disease. *Neurology*, **34**, 939–44.

Mendez, M.F., Turner, J., Gilmore, G.C., *et al.* (1990) Balint's Syndrome in Alzheimer's Disease: visuospatial functions. *International Journal of Neuroscience*, **54** (3–4), 339–46.

Miner, G.D. (ed.) (1989) *Caring for Alzheimer's Patients: A Guide for Family and Health Care Workers*, Insight Books, Plenum Press, New York.

Mullan, M. (1991) A genetic defect causing Alzheimer's Disease. Editorial. *British Journal of Hospital Medicine*, **45**, 131.

Neary, D. and Snowden, J.S. (1990) The differential diagnosis of dementias caused by neurodegenerative disease. *Seminars The Neurosciences*, **2**, 81–8.

O'Keefe, S.T. (1994) Rating the severity of delirium: The Delirium Assessment Scale. *International Journal of Geriatric Psychiatry*, **9**, 551–6.

Orrell, M.W., Sahakian, B.J. and Bergmann, K. (1989) Self neglect and frontal lobe dysfunction. *British Journal of Psychiatry*, **155**, 101–5.

Orrell, M.W. and Sahakian, B.J. (1991) Dementia of the frontal lobe type. *Psychological Medicine*, **21**, 553–6.

Prencipe, M. and Marini, C. (1989) Leuko-araiosis: definition and clinical correlates – an overview. *European Neurology*, **29**(Suppl. 2), 27–9.

Roberts, G., Gentleman, S., Lynch, A. Graham D. (1991) A4 Amyloid protein deposition in the brain after head trauma. *The Lancet*, **338**, 1422–3.

St George-Hyslop, P., Tanzi, R., Polinsky, R. *et al.* (1987) The genetic defect causing Alzheimer's disease maps on chromosome 21. *Science*, **235**, 885–90.

Trzepacz, P.T., Baker, R.W. and Greenhouse, J. (1988) A symptom rating scale for delirium. *Psychiatry Research*, **23**, 89–97.

Van Duijn, C.M. and Hofman, A. (1991) Relation between nicotine intake and Alzheimer's Disease. *British Medical Journal*, **302**, 1491–4.

Verfaellie, M., Rapcsak, S.Z. and Heilman, K.M. (1990) Impaired shifting of attention in Balint's Syndrome. *Brain Cognition*, **12**(2), 195–204.

Wilcock, G.K. (1983) Age and Alzheimer's Disease. *The Lancet*, 6 August, 346.

Wilcock, G.K. (1988) Recent research into dementia. *Age and Ageing*, **17**, 73–86.

Whittaker, J.J. (1989) Postoperative confusion in the elderly. *International Journal of Geriatric Psychiatry*, **4**, 321–6.

4

More 'new' dementias

Although many of the newly identified conditions require further clarification and there are ragged edges which suggest a possible overlap, there is also considerable difficulty experienced by allied professions in understanding all the implications of the highly specialized research findings of their colleagues in the fields of biochemistry, neuropathology and neurobiology! Even so it is vital for those working with older people to have some appreciation of developments and possible explanations for behaviours and conditions met in practice. Errors are frequently made in misunderstanding behaviour due to specific functional impairments, but it can prove equally disastrous to mistake or overlook the symptoms and signs of a particular neurodegenerative disorder and provide inappropriate treatment. The amount of information now available in the literature regarding specific brain disorders is sufficient to inspire a more careful consideration of presenting difficulties and more relevant treatment programmes, designed not for the masses, but for the individual.

SUB-CORTICAL CONDITIONS

Albert, Feldman and Willis proposed the concept of sub-cortical dementia in 1974. It took several years before this was accepted in practice, and even now it is not always regarded as totally separate from the obviously cortical disorders (Hodges, 1993). However, most treatable dementias exhibit subcortical patterns, and to ignore cognitive aspects can only result in inadequate treatment and management. Although sub-cortical dementia no longer falls into the category of 'new' dementias, some of the recently identified conditions do and in order to assist those still unsure of the characteristics of subcortical states a brief outline will be offered here. More in depth coverage can be found in publications by Peretz and Cummings (in Holden, 1988), Hodges (1993) and Cummings (1990).

The initial formulation was as a result of careful investigations of a patient with **Progressive Supranuclear Palsy** or PSP (see below). Albert *et al.* (1974) proposed that sub-cortical dementia consisted of:

- memory disorders;

- a slowing down of action and thought;
- personality changes, apathy and inertia;
- no evidence of apraxia, agnosia or aphasia (although dysarthria occurred).

The signs have been refined and now consist of:

- disturbed attention and concentration;
- slowness of mental processing;
- forgetfulness, rather than true memory loss;
- particular kinds of cognitive impairment;
- personality changes;
- visuospatial disturbances;
- absence of agnosia, aphasia and apraxia;
- an associated motor disorder.

Neuropsychological investigations will focus on these deficits.

Patients with a sub-cortical dementia exhibit severe physical rather than neuropsychological signs. Their cognitive abilities are more 'dilapidated' than damaged and their mental abilities are often underestimated because of their slow response. From the early stages of the illness they have difficulty in reading and possibly calculation. Reading problems are not due to an inability to read and could be explained by the length of time it takes them to complete a line, so that when the end is reached the person has lost his or her place and can start a new line either above or below the right one. Working through mathematical problems is also at a slow pace, probably causing similar difficulties – losing the thread. Later in the disease process tests for frontal lobe function will be failed. EEG is often normal and a CT scan may only show non-specific atrophy, though PET shows frontal abnormalities and SPET helps to differentiate frontal lobe dementia by revealing anterior sub-cortical abnormalities with preserved frontal areas.

Memory will appear impaired, but it is advisable to perservere and, through encouragement and patience, response may improve, demonstrating a dilapidated memory rather than a true memory loss.

The commonest sub-cortical disorders are:

- Parkinson's disease, with loss of neurones in the substantia nigra;
- Huntington's Chorea, with neuronal loss in the corpus stratum, and damage to the caudate nucleus and putamen;
- Progressive Supranuclear Palsy (PSP), which involves the nuclei of the brain stem and is a much rarer condition.

PSP, or the Steele–Richardson–Olzewski syndrome, is distinguished by supranuclear ophthalmoplegia – eyes that are unable to look downwards or follow movement. On a request to look in one direction the person usually looks to the opposite side, even though the head is turned correctly and, when leaning forward, the eyes turn upwards. The eyes have a staring look to them. Obviously this causes problems in walking about and the person appears to have a gait disturbance. Fear of falling over something can be the cause, but a disturbance in balance can be present. Rigidity, neck stiffness and an upturned head are other signs easily observed. Pseudo-bulbar palsy is usually present – a masked facial expression, dysarthria, drooling and an open mouth are common. The person may become mute eventually. Neuropsychological signs are as previously stated. The person's ability is often underestimated. This condition affects people in the 45–75 age range and progresses to death in 2 to 10 years.

Other sub-cortical dementias include **Wilson's Disease**, which is an inherited abnormality in the metabolism of copper that results in toxic accumulations of it in the liver, brain, eye and other organs. It can occur at any age, though its course is more rapid in youth. The neuropsychological dysfunctions are those outlined above, but neurological disorders include rigidity, tremor, inco-ordination, dysarthria, drooling, dysphagia (difficulty swallowing) and a mask-like face. Almost invariably the 'Kayser–Fleischer' rings – green, yellow or brown copper deposits – appear in the cornea of the eye.

Children and young adults can suffer from **Friedreich's ataxia** and other conditions such as **olivopontocerebellar atrophy**, though the latter can appear around the age of 50 years. These are degenerative diseases of the nervous system, mainly genetic; gait and postural disturbances are a common feature with dysarthria, disorders of vision and muscle weakness accompanying features. These are described in detail by Holden (1988).

Recent literature suggests that neurobehavioural impairment in multiple sclerosis has a similar pattern to sub-cortical dementia (Hodges, 1993), but it is remarkable that so little attention has been paid to older people suffering from **AIDS**, the acquired immune-deficiency syndrome which precipitates a sub-cortical condition.

Aids

The cumulative totals at the end of January 1994 for age groups in Scotland up to 69 years of age are given in Table 4.1 and the totals in the UK for those up to 65 years (CD(S) Unit 1994) are given in Table 4.2.

AIDS is another condition which demonstrates the existence of dementia with age groups other than the over 60s. However, it is alarming to note the number of cases of AIDS in the older population which strongly suggests that there could well be a considerable number of undetected or misdiagnosed cases as well. The sudden drop of numbers from the 50 year groups to those in the 60 year ones cannot simply imply that death is the only reason.

Table 4.1 HIV infected persons in Scotland

60–64	= 7 males 0 females
65–69	= 4 males 1 female
However 50–59	= 43 males 6 females
Total infected	= 2055 in 1994 (all ages)

Table 4.2 UK cases of AIDS and HIV-1

Age	Male		Female		Unknown	Total	
	AIDS	HIV-1	AIDS	HIV-1	HIV-1	AIDS	HIV-1
55–59	258	279	7	20	—	265	299
60–64	126	157	2	5	—	128	162
65+	70	85	7	11	1	77	97
All ages	7840	17802	687	2721	20	8518	20543

Equally alarming are the figures implicating children where positive HIV is found due to congenital factors or blood transfusions: UK totals 0–14 years = 643 (AIDS: 76 males and 61 females; HIV-1: 379 males and 129 females). Unfortunately there is a rise in the number of adolescent cases and the level of risk for this group is rapidly increasing (Boyer and Kegeles, 1991). These figures for younger generations could well indicate a steady increase in the numbers of young people who suffer from a dementing process.

This tragic condition has been extensively studied for neuropsychiatric factors, particularly by Navia and colleagues (1986a, 1986b), whose detailed reports have demonstrated the existence of an AIDS dementia complex (ADC), a term now in regular use. In their studies they identified a third of their subjects at various stages of ADC. Table 4.3 lists signs of ADC.

Navia *et al.* (1986a, 1986b) and others concluded that one third of AIDS patients showed mild ADC initially and in the later stages two thirds had a more serious ADC. Tross *et al.* (1988) also confirmed the sub-cortical pattern. Neuropsychological deficits showing poor response are:

Visuospatial ability.
Sequencing.
Motor tests.
Manipulation of acquired knowledge.
Abstracting ability.
Speed of response.
Aphasia, agnosia and true amnesia are absent.

Table 4.3 Signs of ADC

Early signs of ADC: forgetfulness loss of concentration subjective confusion slowness of thought loss of balance apathy social withdrawal. motor impairments could also occur, and behavioural abnormalities were not uncommon
Later developments: increasing cognitive dysfunction mutism, paralysis, incontinence severe dementia CT scan showed cortical atrophy and ventricular enlargement PET showed thalamic and basal ganglia involvement A predominately sub-cortical pattern of deterioration

Although Katona (1989) and Treisman *et al.* (1993) have provided an overview of the relevant literature on AIDS, information on the effects, changes and needs of older victims is extremely hard to find. What little there is notes that misdiagnosis is common and that 75% die within three months of diagnosis. The strange belief that homosexuals do not grow old can be dismissed by one report showing that 35 out of 65 over 65 year olds with AIDS were Gay. Another report stated vaguely that older AIDS victims were much more aggressive. It would be of interest to know more about the circumstances in which such a conclusion was made!

AIDS and older people is a subject which demands more information in order to assist care and health workers to identify the needs and treatment required.

Peter Reed retired three years ago when he was 65. He was an excellent chef in a well known restaurant. His history was clouded with mystery. The staff thought he had been married when he was a young man, but there was no sign of a family and he did not appear to have any friends who could throw any light on his past. At work he had been aloof, friendly enough, but not sociable. He was meticulous, responsible and only occasionally bad-tempered.

Recently he visited his GP complaining that he felt tired, had bouts of incontinence and difficulty in concentration. The community nurse visited him and found that his house was rather unkempt and when she asked him to show her where she could make a cup of tea for them both, he became angry and distressed. His kitchen was in minor disorder, not in keeping with his previous concern for organization and, even when he calmed down, he could not remember where things were stored and took a long time to put the kettle on. His conversation was normal and his knowledge of current events was good. She felt that he was depressed and lonely so she offered to contact one of the local Age Concern social groups for him. He was not pleased.

With so little information with which to make a diagnosis of AIDS, GPs and home visiting staff are faced with a real problem of how to investigate without causing indignation, fear or even a catastrophic reaction. However, each situation must be carefully considered for such a possibility and very sensitive means to investigate a possible ADC must be found.

Vascular sub-cortical conditions

As stated in the previous chapter, strokes can occur in the sub-cortex, but unfortunately they are frequently overlooked and there is little general understanding of their nature. When infarction occurs in large vessels cortical dysfunction usually results, but when occlusion involves many small vessels dysfunction is sub-cortical. Strokes in the sub-cortex are usually called lacunar strokes, infarcts or dementia.

- Lacuna – a small cavity within a structure, especially boney tissue.
- Lacunae, which are small in size, are ischemic infarcts in deeper parts of the brain and brainstem
- Lacunar state – a pseudo-bulbar disorder, small strokes cause smooth walled cavities in brain tissue.
- Pseudobulbar palsy – dysarthria, dysphagia, facial movement impairments, upper motor neurone problems, and sometimes hemipareisis and short-step gait.

Sub-cortical vascular accidents, or lacunar strokes, are often regarded as the same thing as Binswanger's disease. It is important to stress that the presence of lacunae does not necessarily indicate a dementing condition. It would seem that the severity and distribution of white matter changes separate those people with resultant dementia with only a few lacunae found at post mortem, from those who, despite the presence of leukoaraiosis (LA) or lacunar infarcts, remained intellectually normal. Recent findings have shown that it is not the amount of infarction, but the area where infarctions occur which is critical. To quote

> 'It is probably only the combination of severity and distribution of white matter changes that distinguishes the intellectually normal patient with LA or lacunar infarcts from the patient with severe dementia'.
>
> BROWN, 1993

Marie (1901) was probably the first researcher to describe lacunar states: **etat lacunaire** was an accumulation of sub-cortical lacunae leading to a dementia, pseudobulbar palsy and small stepped gait (marche a petit pas). Lacunar syndromes take several forms, perhaps the commonest being Binswanger's Disease.

Binswanger's disease

Otto Binswanger was Professor of Neuropsychiatry in Jena, 1882–1919. He coined the term **encephalitis subcorticalis chronica progressiva** in 1894 at the same meeting in Dresden when Alzheimer introduced arteriosclerotic brain atrophy. Alzheimer (1902) and Franz Nizzl (1920) gave this concept its eponymous title and Olszewski (1962) brought it back into the limelight.

Binswanger's disease; or subcortical arteriosclerotic encephalopathy, is a progressive syndrome due to injury to deep white matter of the cerebral hemispheres. Onset is at 50 to 70 years. There is typically a history of stroke-like episodes in hypertensive patients. Remissions and plateaus occur, but it is progressive and accumulative over 3 to 10 years. The symptoms are listed in Table 4.4.

Table 4.4 Symptoms of Biswanger's disease

Acute strokes
Motor signs – wide-based gait, small steps
Pseudo-bulbar palsy
Defective judgement
Apathy, slow responses (bradyphrenia)
Emotional lability – euphoria, aggression, depression
Perseveration
Poor drive, poor memory
Dysarthria
Visuo-spatial deficits
Dilapidated thinking

There is deep white matter damage to the frontal, parietal and occipital lobes and small infarctions in the basal ganglia, thalamus and pons. There is **no** Aphasia, Apraxia or Agnosia – a sub-cortical pattern. Diagnosis can be assisted by PET, SPECT or MRI scans. Leukoaraiosis (LA) shows up on CT and particularly on MRI scans. Its presence in about 30% of apparent AD patients may cause difficulties in diagnosis, though researchers are seeking explanations for this.

Binswanger's remains a controversial issue, but CT and MRI scans which show severe LA in the periventricular regions have helped to demonstrate that it is not as uncommon as previously believed. LA is non-age-related and present in a variety of conditions irrespective of the presence or absence of a dementia, even in healthy, normal elderly subjects (Brown, 1993).

Drug therapy can improve the course of vascular dementia, particularly if the associated physical and psychological conditions are treated symptomatically, but there is a great need for more clarification of the implications of LA, its relationship to dementia and a need for improved methods of diagnosis – particularly of the sub-cortical vascular conditions.

Paramedian thalamic infarct

Paramedian thalamic infarct is a good example of a condition that can develop as a result of minor infarction. These are so small that they may not be picked up by the CT scan. The symptoms are listed in Table 4.5.

Table 4.5 Symptoms of paramedian thalamic infarct

Sudden onset of confusion
Disturbances of consciousness
Fluctuating vigilance
Coma
Hypersomnia
Ocularmotor disturbance:
vertical gaze paralysis
third nerve palsy
poor convergence
Neuropsychological signs:
amnesia
poor attention
behavioural changes
poor long term memory
Thalamic amnesia
Sub-cortical pattern

Katz, Alexander and Mandell (1987) and Arboix, Marti-Vitalta and Garcia (1990) found MRI scanning much superior in demonstrating small lesions. From a neuropsychological viewpoint a valuable contribution has been provided by Wolfe *et al.* (1990), who employed a number of frontal tests with patients who were found to have two or more lacunae and no cortical infarction, furthermore the vast majority of the subjects were not demented. Results of tests sensitive to frontal lobe damage showed errors with patients who had multiple lacunar infarctions, even though there was no evidence of dementia. The tests proving to be the most sensitive did not include all frontal type assessments, but did include:

- Stroop Colour Interference Test;
- Visual-Verbal Test (shifting mental set);

- California Verbal Learning Test (executive function);
- Verbal fluency

The subjects showed apathetic behaviour. Wolfe *et al.* (1990) concluded that the subjects with multiple lacunar infarcts fell into the frontal lobe disorder category of apathetic, lethargic and lacking in spontaneity rather than the type where restlessness, impulsivity and hyperkinetic responses are characteristic. They suggest that 'there is a stage between dementia and normal in which multiple subcortical lacunar infarctions produce signs of impairment of frontal systems'.

CORTICO-SUB-CORTICAL ENCEPHALOPATHIES

Lewy body disease

Frederic H. Lewy (1885–1950) came from Berlin where he studied medicine and later worked in Alzheimer's neuropathology laboratory in Munich. He became interested in the 'shaking palsy' and published important papers on his findings. After serving as a soldier in the German army in 1914–18, he returned to his research in Berlin and in 1934 emigrated to the USA where he became Professor of Neuroanatomy and Neuropathology in Pennsylvania. In 1912 he identified elongated structures in certain nerve cells of patients suffering from Parkinson's disease and in 1919 Tretiakoff named them after him. These **Lewy bodies** (LBs) are microscopic structures found in the neurones of Parkinson disease patients in the pigmented nuclei of the brain stem, particularly the substantia nigra; others, such as the locus coeruleus and raphe nuclei, are also involved. The classical description of them is 'intracytoplasmic eosinophilic (pink staining) hyaline inclusions' associated with incipient or progressive degeneration; they are single, round and surrounded by a halo of filaments.

Until recent years, cortical LBs were not identified by investigations, probably because they are slightly different from those found in the sub-cortex. However a new technique revealed that LBs also occur in the cortex and the Japanese school (Kosaka *et al.*, 1984) precipitated a line of investigation which has led to the concept of a cortico-sub-cortical condition with a confusing nosology, but which will be referred to here as Lewy body disease (LBD).

One of the many controversial issues surrounding LBD is what it should be called. Kosaka *et al.* (1984) classified it into three types:

- group A, diffuse LBD, widespread cortical LBs plus AD changes;
- group B, transitional LBD but fewer LBs than A;
- group C, essentially Parkinsonian (PD), with LBs in the sub-cortex.

By 1990 Kosaka revised his views and suggested that there were only two forms:

- DLBD (diffuse LBD) without AD pathology, but with PD;
- DLBD with AD pathology.

In Great Britain two major schools researched the condition. In Newcastle between 1982 and 1987 the Perrys and their colleagues (Perry *et al.*, 1990a) examined 93 necropsies, concentrating on patients who were 70+ years at death and who had suffered from a dementia. They found 20% with senile dementia Lewy body type (SDLT). In Nottingham, Byrne *et al.*, (1989) examined 216 brains from one year of necropsies, 55 of whom had had a dementing condition and identified 15 of these with LBD.

In San Diego Hansen and Galasko (1992) used the term Lewy body variant (LBV).

Perry *et al.*, (1989) suggested another classification:

- diffuse LBD
- PD and dementia
- PD without dementia
- atypical – SDLT
- AD + PD.

The studies from Newcastle noted that although there were senile plaques similar to AD present, there were few if any neurofibrillary tangles. There was no evidence of a familial factor. The neuronal loss in LBD was 40% in comparison to the 80% in AD. Hallucinations, particularly visual ones, and paranoid delusions were common presenting symptoms. The authors concluded that LBD was a different condition from AD and that LBD was the second commonest dementing condition, more frequent than vascular disease dementias.

Several studies using the new technique to identify cortical LBs showed that PD patients also had cortical LBS that had not been previously noted (Schmidt *et al.*, 1991; Hughes *et al.*, 1992; Perry *et al.*, 1990a). Operational criteria for LBD proposed by McKeith *et al.* (1992) reported that cognitive impairment was usually more preserved than the level associated with a dementia, and, that behavioural disturbances were less of a problem initially.

Although it is necessary to be aware of the symptoms and signs of LBD (Table 4.6) in order to be able to distinguish it from other degenerative conditions, it is also useful to have some knowledge of the probable course, which is outlined in Table 4.7. The picture may be obscured by neuroleptic drugs. However, recent studies have shown that subjects not on drugs also had extrapyramidal disorders (Ballard *et al.*, 1993). There follows a progressive decline over many months ending in death due to cardiac or pulmonary disease. Neuroleptic drugs appear to hasten the decline and can prove dangerous. Parkinson's disease is a common accompaniment.

Table 4.6 Clinical features of Lewy, body disease

Fluctuating cognitive impairment: memory impairment visuo-spatial ability logical thought probably some language disorder (comprehension and naming are preserved, but syntax error and perseveration result in incoherent speech) copying and drawing can also be impaired
Clouding of consciousness, very variable and episodic, often reported as TIAs, becoming more frequent in time
Visual hallucinations – often worse at night
Auditory hallucinations
Paranoid delusions
Depression
Repeated unexplained falls – interpreted as 'fits', but no corroborative evidence
Mild spontaneous extrapyramidal features – could be related to drugs, but patients not on any medication have been found to have these changes
The fluctuating condition persists, often rapidly progressing to severe dementia
Neuroleptic sensitivity
There is no underlying physical condition
There is no previous history of strokes, though Parkinson's disease may be present

Table 4.7 Clinical course of LBD

1st Stage
1–3 years prior to investigation: some forgetfulness, though this is more a lapse of concentration. If a physical illness occurred there would probably have been an accompanying delirium, followed by an apparent full recovery. However, others may notice a subsequent mental and physical decline.
2nd Stage
First examination. More sustained cognitive changes present, but of a **fluctuating** nature. All other symptoms now obvious.
3rd Stage
Sudden increase in confusion, psychosis and behavioural disturbances – shouting, aggressive on approach and persistent delirium. Family unable to cope – exhausted.

Liza Collins (72) comes from a long living family. She has been an active, cheerful woman of good intelligence with a loving family. Despite various moves of her children to different parts of the country, and even abroad, they all remain in close touch. The daughter who resides nearby has not been called upon to supply great support for Mrs Collins as she has remained alert, independent and socially involved.

However, recent events have caused the family to gather at home in a state of alarm. Mrs Collins had begun to ring her daughter more frequently, each time sounding fearful and angry. She claims that there are people trying to get in through a window, or standing outside making rude gestures and threatening her. The police have been called out and eventually the daughter and her husband stayed the night to see for themselves what was happening. Mrs Collins suddenly jumped to her feet and began screaming at a window and then became angry with the younger couple because they would not make a move to defend her against something or someone they could not see.

Other family members have stayed with their mother for several days and have noted that most of the time she is perfectly normal, but at some point during the day she has become terribly confused; sometimes she appears to be hallucinating, but it has been the cognitive changes that have caused them most concern. During these episodes she has been unsteady on her feet and has had a few falls. They are all worried about her ability to continue living alone and are anxious to know exactly what is wrong.

With LBD there appears to be a fairly consistent pattern of neurotransmitter activity: a reduction in dopamine (not as severe as in PD) and cholinergic activities whereas serotinergic activity is normal when hallucinations are present (Perry *et al.*, 1990b). This produces an imbalance and it is this imbalance on which research is concentrating in order to discover a means to treat the condition and reverse it. It seems possible that LBD patients could respond well to cholinergic therapy once it is perfected. The identification of LBD and the possibilities of treatment are some of the most exciting findings within recent years.

Several studies (McKeith *et al.*, 1992) have noted that there is a danger in the use of neuroleptics which can provoke irreversible, adverse reactions, including extrapyramidal side effects, which can have a fatal outcome. In comparison to AD patients on neuroleptic drugs LBD patients have been found to exhibit more side effects and have a shorter life expectancy than the AD patients.

Neuroleptic malignant syndrome

Neuroleptic malignant syndrome (NMS) has been studied by groups other than those concerned with LBD. Nicklason, Finucane and Pathy (1991) reviewed the scanty literature stressing the lethal nature of NMS and the rarity of its recognition in older people. They stressed the need for early diagnosis and outlined the symptoms:

- akinesis
- muscle rigidity
- hyperthermia
- autonomic instability
- altered consciousness.

It is suggested that NMS is due to central dopamine antagonism and the introduction of neuroleptic agents. It can occur even with infants and the number affected after the age of 65 years is probably greatly underestimated. The mortality rate is 16–24% and a delay in diagnosis can have serious results.

To aid early recognition and treatment, Nicklason *et al.* recommended the following course of action: the neuroleptic drug and replace with, e.g. dopamine agonists such as L-dopa or bromocriptine, to induce muscle relaxation;

- provide supportive care;
- reduce hyperthermia by sponging;
- maintain fluid and electrolytes;
- treat any infection.

When LBD is present there appears to be evidence to suggest that NMS is a matter of concern. McKeith *et al.* (1992) noted that over 50% of the subjects in their study who suffered from LBD and who were prescribed standard doses of neuroleptic drugs showed 'acute and often irreversible adverse reactions indicative of a neuroleptic malignant syndrome'. A fatal outcome was common, survival rates being much lower than with those patients diagnosed as suffering from AD, furthermore those that survived often developed side effects including extrapyramidal symptoms.

The importance of discovering the existence of LBD is not to be underestimated. Although research is incomplete, it would seem that there is a spectrum of LBD which includes PD and other forms and may have some, as yet unclear, relationship with AD. Although these relationships remain unclear LBD is being recognized as a common form of dementia and one that requires a different approach from other conditions (Perry *et al.*, 1991; Byrne, 1992). It is possible that future treatment will reverse or contain it.

LBD has a fluctuating course so it requires that the patient is treated:

- with acceptance of retained abilities, even though functioning may vary;
- with explanations regarding possible hallucinations during lucid periods;
- without neuroleptic drugs;
- at home for as long as possible;
- as a normal, sensible individual during lucid periods.

It will assist the attitude and understanding of carers and probably simplify arrangements and approaches and it will provide professionals with a reason to be positive.

In investigating the problem, the changes outlined above in the list of signs and symptoms must be considered. The fluctuating course, even from hour to hour, will be important, but to differentiate between AD and LBD further – the memory loss is not present in LBD and the results of mental test scores will vary according to the fluctuations of confusion, although usually LBD patients will perform better. Several drug therapies are presently under investigation for the treatment of LBD; chlormethiazal has been used successfully to control the symptoms of a very small group of patients, but it is far too early to be satisfied by these findings, despite the promise. However, the identification of several 'new' causes of dementia is opening doors to better understanding, more hope for successful treatments and more detailed information for future research with a positive, practical outcome in view.

MULTI-FOCAL ENCEPHALOPATHIES OR PRION DISEASE

Unlike the encephalopathies outlined previously, these multi-focal types cause severe neurological, or physical, and cognitive changes. These conditions have suddenly come into focus. For many years they were given a variety of names: transmissible viruses, transmissible spongiform encephalopathies, unconventional viral infections or slow viruses. The disease was transmitted in a number of ways usually requiring infected tissue, although in some cases there appeared to be a genetic form. Prion diseases affect both animals and man.

Animal prion disease

- Scrapie – sheep and goats;
- feline spongiform encephalopathy – cats;
- chronic wasting disease – mule deer and elk;
- exotic ungulate encephalopathy – nyala and kudu;
- bovine spongiform encephalopathy – cattle;
- transmissible mink encephalopathy – mink;
- murine spongiform encephalopathy – mice.

Scrapie has been known for probably over 200 years. It was thought that the condition was passed on by an infected animal rubbing itself against the fences around the field and another scratching itself in the same place. This may have some bearing on transmission as non-infected sheep, when introduced into pastures where infected sheep previously grazed, developed the condition. However, it is referred to as a natural disease and a genetic element is suspected to be a major factor. Mink encephalopathy appears to be related to the animals biting each other whilst eating scrapie infected food. Of course bovine spongiform encephalopathy, or BSE, is probably the best known of all prion diseases in Britain and probably would not have arisen if cattle had been fed in a normal manner. For some reason the rendered carcasses of scrapie infected sheep were introduced as a dietary supplement with the resultant tragic effects. Unfortunately the disease has been passed on to the calves. Debate continues on the method of transmission and its implications. Feline spongiform encephalopathy, chronic wasting disease and exotic ungulate encephalopathy are probably also caused by ingestion of prion contaminated food.

Human prion diseases

The early accounts of transmissible viruses usually referred to Jakob-Creutzfeldt or Creutzfeldt–Jakob's Disease and Kuru (Gajdusek 1977; Traub, 1983). Cummings and Benson (1992) provided a detailed account of the disease processes that are now recognized as prion diseases. These include:

- Jakob–Creutzfeldt disease (sporadic and familial)
- Gerstmann–Straussler–Scheinker disease
- Kuru
- Fatal Familial Insomnia.

Essentially these diseases prove fatal and until recently had received little research attention with the result that understanding was limited. **Jakob–Creutzfeldt disease** (JCD) is rare, affecting 0.5–1.0 per million worldwide, the onset is usually in the 60/70s, but affected 18–20 year olds have been reported. It is 10–15% familial and affects both sexes. It progresses rapidly – 50% die within six months, 75–90% within one year; occasionally the familial course may be 2–16 years. Familial cases have an earlier onset and a more protracted course than sporadic cases. The signs and symptoms are listed in Table 4.8.

Creutzfeldt described his findings in 1920 and Jakob identified the same condition the following year, but the disease was not really the focus of interest until Gajdusek had identified a similar picture with Kuru.

Table 4.8 Signs and symptoms of Jacob-Creutzfeldt disease

Initially – vague physical discomfort, apprehension, fatigue, poor sleep, appetite changes, poor concentration, forgetfulness and depression
Within weeks – cortical, pyramidal and extrapyramidal signs appear, plus aphasia, agnosia, apraxia, hallucinations, delusions and a severe cognitive deterioration
Neurological signs are numerous – myoclonus, pyramidal signs, cerebellar ataxia or extrapyramidal features
EEG is supposedly characteristic, but often found too late
There is much variability in the clinical features
The cerebral cortex appears spongiform and there are other neuropathological changes
Eventually (after months or weeks) – vegetative state, leading to death.

Early, much quoted examples of Jakob–Creutzfeldt's disease (JCD) included transmissions via a cornea graft from an infected donor, the use of an ineffectual sterilization of depth electrodes used in the treatment of epilepsy in two 18 year olds and the consumption of sheep's eyes which was a dubious delicacy for a North African tribe. More recently the transmission via sheep's eye has become suspect as an enterprising researcher traced the origins of the tribe back over generations to a family from a European town where JCD was common. More recently, pituitary derived growth hormone from human cadavers has led to 10 (to date) out of 1908 individuals in the UK developing JCD.

It was always accepted that person to person contact was not a problem, but that the possibility of contaminated tissue should always be considered. Careful handling of any tissue from such patients and great care with any instruments was strongly advised. The dangers of transmissible viruses were first appreciated as a result of Gajdsek's work in Papua, New Guinea on Kuru (Gajdusek, 1977).

By using human infected brain tissue it has been demonstrated that the disease can be transmitted to laboratory animals. There is a high incidence of the familial form in certain areas of Slovakia and Hungary as well as among Libyan-born Jews. Sadly, to date, there is no cure for this terrible disease.

Kuru was a disease that struck the Fore tribe who inhabited the eastern highlands of New Guinea. Gajdusek began studying the problem in the 1950s and found that patients suffered from headaches, sickness and limb pains, later developing tremor, ataxia and accompanied speech and walking difficulties. A progressive mental deterioration led to death within 12 months. Spongiform changes were found in the brain at autopsy. Kuru had claimed the lives of 50% of the female population, but children of both sexes were also affected. Usually the men were free from it. There were three possible explanations: genetic predisposition, a transmissible source or cannibalism. Apparently women and children ate the brain of the cadavers and men muscle only. Gajdusek must have been a very brave man to inform them of his findings and live to tell the tale! It is notable that Kuru is now a rare condition!

Gerstmann–Straussler–Scheinker disease (GSSD) was first discribed by Gerstmann in 1928, and in 1936 the three researchers provided more detail about members of an Austrian family. Onset is at 20–70 years, death in 4–10 years. It is usually familial (probably autosomal dominant inheritance). The clinical course is described in Table 4.9. The CT scans are normal or show cerebellar atrophy. MRI scans are more helpful while EEG is of little assistance. The course is more protracted than for JCD.

Table 4.9 Clinical course of Gerstmann–Straussler–Scheinker disease

early signs: progressive cerebellar ataxia, inco-ordination, dysarthria, supranuclear gaze palsy, impaired pursuit eye movements;
cognitive changes: middle–late stage–dementia, depression, psychosis;
gradual short term memory impairment, psychomotor retardation, mild anomia, disorientation and poor judgement;
rigidity and bradykinesis.

Although GSSD is similar to JCD it differs by having large numbers of multicentric amyloid plaques in the cerebral and cerebellar hemispheres and less spongiform change or neuronal loss in the grey matter. Several papers have provided accounts of different families demonstrating gross intellectual changes from the age of 20–30 years (Baker, Ridley and Crowe, 1985; Collinge *et al.*, 1989; Tateishi *et al.*, 1988) and involving several generations.

Two other rare diseases – **Fatal Familial Insomnia** and **Alper's Disease**, the former concerning patients of 40–50 years and the latter infants and children – have recently been identified (Medori, Tritschler and Le Blanc, 1992; Cummings and Benson, 1992).

Bovine Spongiform Encephalopathy was possibly one of the precipitants for the flow of papers on the subject of prion disease and in a tragic way has enabled research to find answers and new pathways to better understanding of some extremely distressing and, at present, fatal conditions. Most of the research has provided specialized neuropathological and biochemical material which can prove very difficult to follow for members of other professions. However, there are a few articles in which efforts have been made to present the material in an easier form (Clinton and Wyn Roberts, 1992; Pablos-Mendez, Netto and Dejendini; 1993; Jackson, 1994). As the flow of papers and information proceeds the matter will doubtless become simplified.

What are prions?

The term was first coined by Prusiner (1982) to describe the proteinaceous infectious 'particle' that he thought behaved like an intracellular parasite. However, further study has demonstrated that prion protein production is a normal event in healthy brains and is produced throughout life. The normal prion protein is termed $P^{r}P^{c}$ and is located on the short arm of chromosome 20 of a normal cellular gene – a 'housekeeping gene' necessary for the basic functioning of the cells. The abnormal pathological prion – $P^{r}P^{p}$ – probably results from some interference in production or interaction. The mutation can take different forms and precipitate different disease processes; some are inherited and may not make an appearance for many years, others are transmitted. Studies have identified what is called a **species barrier** – the more similar the prion structure is between two animals the easier it is to transmit a prion disease. In view of the concerns about BSE, it is to be hoped that the converse is true, i.e. that the more different the species the less likely transmission will occur.

Aberrant prions are infectious pathogens that differ from bacteria, fungi, parasites, viroids and viruses, both in structure and resultant disease.

'Warrior' cells

Investigations into prions have led some researchers into very promising and positive avenues (Lowe and Mayer, 1992). Most people are aware that the body is capable of producing anti-toxins which help to keep a person reasonably healthy. In the case of neurodegenerative disorders there has been further clarification.

> *To use an analogy from the Wild West, a homestead (the cell) is proceeding with its daily chores ('housekeeping genes') and all is peace. From over the hill comes a bunch of ruffians or Red Indian raiders (disease process), the women and children ('housekeeping genes') withdraw and the strong men (cytoprotective cell stress proteins) come out to protect them. Sometimes the men are not strong enough to contain the onslaught so they have to call in the sheriff and his posse (future methods of introducing more cytoprotective proteins).*

Study of the cell stress response has provided some valuable information. For instance, **ubiquitin** is one of the cell stress response proteins involved in identifying abnormal proteins for destruction (Figure 4.1) and its detection in neurofibrillary tangles of AD and many other disease processes may well lead to the introduction of new therapeutic approaches. The use of ubiquitin in a new staining technique has led to the identification of cortical Lewy bodies and the relationship of ubiquitin

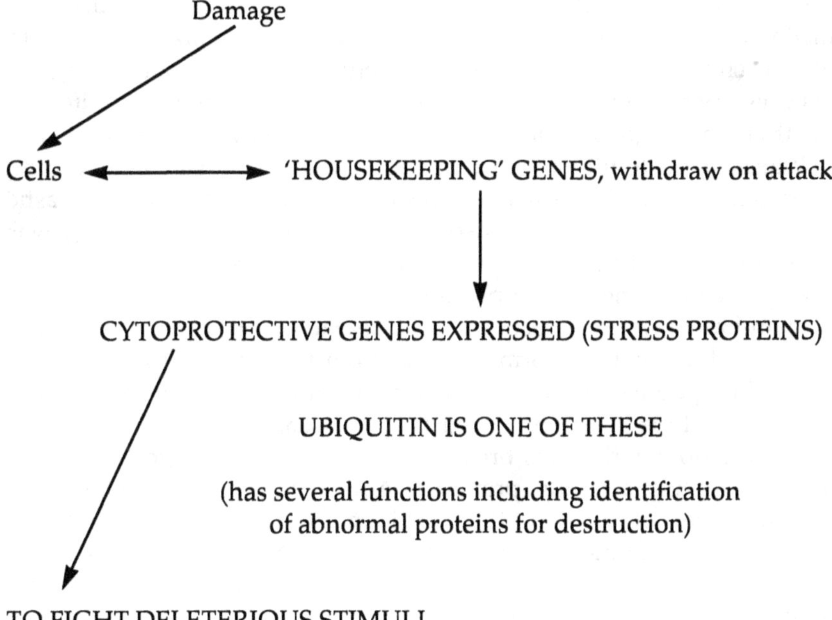

Figure 4.1 'Warrior' cells.

to an enzyme in the Lewy body indicates the presence of a cytoprotective response which could dictate appropriate pharmacological intervention.

These are exciting developments, made even more promising by the possible use of genetic screening, using gene analysis and immunocytochemistry. Many of the conclusions from different research units remain controversial, for instance the belief that prion disease is greatly underestimated has been challenged by Brown *et al.* (1993), but for the moment it is accepted that prion disease and spongiform encephalitis are one and the same.

ENVIRONMENTAL INFLUENCES

There are strong impressions that degenerative conditions could be due to environmental factors. These may have effects in the early years of life and lie dormant for decades before surfacing (Calne *et al.*, 1986). Although the evidence is not conclusive as yet, it is certainly not a matter to dismiss when various situations are examined. The precipitators may be food, gases, ingested foreign substances (e.g. aluminium), unsuspected poisons or trauma such as boxing injuries.

Abiotrophy means that there has been selective, premature decay of functionally related neurones in a specific area of the brain. This could occur in childhood or early adulthood; other neurones could take over the necessary function and eventually become overloaded in later life.

Lathyrism is a good example of this. It is caused by a consistent diet of chick peas and is found in India. Inmates of a prison of war camp during the Second World War developed this complaint, which causes a spastic limb weakness. Many of the prisoners emigrated to Israel after the war and were followed up for 40 years; eventually a large number of them developed a motor neurone type disease.

Guam has become the focus of much research as it would appear that the people there make a form of bread from flour made from the cicad seed. The population can develop a motor neurone/Alzheimer/ Parkinsonian type condition called **Guam disease** even in their forties. There were doubts that this bread could be at fault, though the seed is poisonous unless properly prepared. A further investigation into the possible dangers of the use of this seed identified deaths in parts of Japan and Papua, New Guinea that could be related to the same source – either the juice of the seed was put directly on an open wound to heal it, or a potion was made to act as a tonic.

People who some 30 or 40 years ago had lived in areas where calcium and magnesium were lacking in the soil are now found to be suffering from a motor neurone/Alzheimer/Parkinsonian type of degenerative condition, although living elsewhere. In areas such as Nigeria and Mozambique ataxic myeloneuropathy or subacute parapareis develop and appear to be associated with the consumption of cassava. In Britain there have been concerns about aluminium in the water, toxic substances in the ground and doubts about shellfish from seas where toxins have been dumped.

It has been stated that as man is living longer it is possible that various dangerous substances, foods or industrial emissions may now be more likely to demonstrate their effects than when people died at a younger age. It is already seen as a matter of concern that exhaust emissions from cars are increasing the incidence of asthma at all ages, but it is probable that there are many environmental factors that will be eventually identified as the cause of changes in brain function. On a more positive note, man **is** living longer, so there must be something that is helping this process as well as vice versa!

REFERENCES

Albert, M.L., Feldman, R.G. and Willis, A.L. (1974) The 'subcortical dementia' of progressive supranuclear palsy. *Journal of Neurology, Neurosurgery and Psychiatry*, **37**, 121–30.

Arboix, A., Marti-Vitalta, J.L. and Garcia, J.H. (1990) Clinical study with 227 patients with lacunar infarcts. *Stroke*, **21**(6) 842–7.

Baker, H.F., Ridley, R.M. and Crowe, T.J. (1985) Experimental transmission of an autosomal spongiform encephalopathy: does the infectious agent originate in the human genome? *Clinical Research*, **291**, 299–302.

Ballard, C.G., Mohan, R.N.C., Patel, A. and Bannister, C. (1993) Idiopathic clouding of consciousness – do the patients have Cortical Lewy Body disease? *International Journal of Geriatric Psychiatry*, **8**, 571–6.

Boyer, C.B. and Kegeles, S.M. (1991) AIDS risk and prevention amongst adolescents. *Social Science Medicine*, **33**, 11–23.

Brown, M.M. (1993) Vascular dementia. *Alzheimer's Review*, Vol 3, No. 2, Parke-Davis, Magellan Medical Publishing, London.

Brown, P., Kaur, P., Sulima, M.P., *et al.* (1993) Real and imagined clinicopathological limits of 'prion dementia'. *The Lancet* **341**, No. 8838, 127–9.

Byrne, E.J. (1992) Editorial. Diffuse Lewy Body Disease: spectrum disorder or variety of Alzheimer's Disease. *International Journal of Geriatric Psychiatry*, **7**, 229–34.

Byrne, E.J., Lennox, G., Lowe, J. and Godwin-Austin, R.B. (1989) Diffuse Lewy Body Disease: clinical features in 15 cases. *Journal of Neurology, Neurosurgery and Psychiatry*, **52**, 709–17.

Calne, D.B., Eisen, A., McGeer, E. and Spencer, P. (1986). Alzheimer's Disease, Parkinson's Disease and Motorneurone Disease: Abiotropic interactions between ageing and environment? *The Lancet*, 8 November, 1067–70.

CD(S), Communicable Diseases (Scotland) Unit (1994) *AIDS Scotland*. HMSO, Edinburgh.

Clinton, J. and Wyn Roberts, G. (1992). Editorial. Prion Disease: the essential facts. *International Journal of Geriatric Psychiatry*, **7**, 853–64.

Collinge, J., Harding, A.E., Owen, F., *et al.* (1989) Diagnosis of Gerstmann–Straussler Syndrome in familial dementia with prion protein analysis. *The Lancet*, 1 July, 15–17.

Cummings, J.L. (ed.) (1990) *Subcortical Dementia*, Oxford University Press, Oxford.

Cummings, J.L. and Benson, D.F. (1992) *Dementia: A Clinical Approach*, Butterworth-Heinemann, Boston.

Gajdusek, D.C. (1977) Unconventional viruses and the disappearance of kuru. *Science*, **197**, 340–60.

Hanson, L.A. and Galasko, D. (1992) Lewy Body Disease. *Current Opinion in Neurology and Neurosurgery*, **5**, 889–94.

Hodges, J. (1993) Subcortical Dementia. *Alzheimer's Review* 2 No.3. Parke-Davis, Magellan Medical Publishing, London.

Holden, U.P. (ed.) (1988) *Neuropsychology and Ageing*, Croom Helm, London.

Hughes, A.J., Daniel, S.E., Kilford, L. and Lees, A.J. (1992) Accuracy of clinical diagnosis of idiopathic Parkinson's Disease: a clinico-pathological study of 100 cases. *Journal of Neurology Neurosurgery and Psychiatry*, **55**, 181–4.

Jackson, M. (1994) Prion Diseases *Hospital Update*, February, 71–81.

Katona, C.L.E. (ed.) (1989) *Dementia Disorders: Advances and Prospects*. Chapman & Hall, London.

Katz, D., Alexander, M.P. and Mandell, A.M. (1987) Dementia following strokes in the mesencephalon and diencephalon. *Archives Neurology*, **44**, 560–5.

Kosaka, K. (1990) Diffuse Lewy Body Disease in Japan. *Journal of Neurology*, **237**, 197–204

Kosaka, K. Yoshimura, M., Ikeda, K. and Budka, H. (1984) Diffuse type of Lewy Body Disease: progressive dementia with abundant cortical Lewy Bodies and senile changes of varying degree – a new disease? *Clinical Neuropathology*, **3**, 185–92.

Lowe, J. and Mayer, R.J. (1992) Ubiquitin and the cell stress response in the dementias, in *Psychogeriatrics*, (ed. T. Arie), Churchill Livingstone, Edinburgh.

Marie, P. (1901) Des foyers lacunaires de desintegration et de differents autres etats cavitaires du cerveau. *Review Medica*, **21**, 281–98.

McKeith, I.G., Perry, R.H., Fairburn, A.F., *et al.* (1992) Operational criteria for Senile Dementia of the Lewy Body Type (SDLT). *Psychological Medicine*, **22**, 911–22.

Medori, R., Tritschler, H.-J. and LeBlanc, A. (1992) Fatal familial insomnia, a prion disease with a mutation at codon 178 of the prion protein gene. *New England Journal of Medicine*, **326**, 444–9.

Navia, B.A., Cho, E., Petito, C.K. and Price, R.W. (1986a) The AIDS Dementia complex. 11. Neuropathology. *Annals of Neurology*, **19**, 525.

Navia, B.A., Jordan B.D. and Price, R.W. (1986b) The AIDS Dementia Complex. 1. Clinical Features. *Annals of Neurology*, **19**, 517–23.

Nicklason, F.N., Finucane, P.M. and Pathy, M.S.J. (1991) Neuroleptic Malignant Syndrome – an unrecognized problem in elderly patients with psychiatric illness. *International Journal of Geriatric Psychiatry*, **6**, 171–5.

Olswieski, I. (1962) Subcortical arteriosclerotic encephalopathy: Review of the literature on the so-called Binswanger's Disease and presentation of 2 cases. *World Neurology*, **3**, 359–75.

Pablos-Mendez, A., Netto, E.M. and Defendini, R. (1993) Infectious prions or cytotoxic metabolites. *The Lancet*, 341, No.8838, 159–61.

Perry, R.H., Irving, D., Blessed, G., *et al.* (1989) Senile dementia of the Lewy Body type and spectrum of Lewy Body Disease. *Lancet*, **i**, 1088.

Perry, R.H., Irving, D., Blessed, G., *et al.* (1990a) Senile Dementia of the Lewy Body type. A clinically and neuropathologically distinct form of Lewy Body dementia in the elderly. *Journal of Neurological Science*, **95**, 119–39.

Perry, E.K., Marshall, E., Kerwin, J. *et al.* (1990b) Evidence of monoaminergic-cholinergic imbalance related to visual hallucinations in Lewy Body Dementia. *Journal of Neurochemistry*, **55**, 1454–6.

Perry, E.K., McKeith, I., Thompson, P., *et al.*, (1991) Topography, extent, and clinical relevance of neurochemical deficits in dementia of the Lewy Body type, Parkinson's Disease and Alzheimer's Disease. *Annals of the New York Academy of Sciences*, Vol.640: *Aging and Alzheimer's Disease*.

Prusiner, S.B. (1982) Novel proteinaceous infectious particles cause scrapie. *Science*, **216**, 136–44.

Schmidt, M.L., Murray, L., Lee, V.M.-Y., *et al.* (1991) Epitope map of neurofilament protein domains in cortical and peripheral nervous system Lewy Bodies. *American Journal of Pathology*, **139**, 53–65.

Tateishi, J., Kitamoto, T., Hasigushi, H. and Shii, H. (1988) Gerstmann–Straussler–Scheinker Disease: immunohistological and experimental studies. *American Neurological Association*, **24**, 35–40.

Traub, R.D. (1983) Recent data and hypotheses on Creutzfeldt–Jakob Disease, in *The Dementias, Advances in Neurology*, Vol.38, (eds R. Mayeux and W.G. Rosen), Raven Press, New York.

Treisman, G., Lyketos, C., Fishman, M. and Folstein, M. (1993) Neuropsychiatric research on HIV-infected patients. *Current Opinion in Psychiatry*, **6**, 96–100.

Tross, S., Price, R.W. and Navia, B. (1988) Neuropsychological characterization of the AIDS Dementia Complex: a preliminary report. *AIDS*, **2**, 81.

Wolfe, N., Linn, R., Babikian, V.L., *et al.* (1990) Frontal system impairments following multiple lacunar infarcts. *Archives Neurology*, **47**, 129–32.

5

Head injury and older people

Gerontology is still a new science and it is only within recent years that a more positive approach to the problems which arise amongst older people has been investigated. Tremendous changes in belief, attitude and treatment have occurred, but there are many areas as yet untouched or just vaguely addressed. Head injury continues to be a subject which is given far too little attention by health authorities and government officers despite the excellent research and innovations provided by several specialist units. Work with adults and children has provided improved insight into the difficulties faced by the individual and the relatives, but, unfortunately, the guidelines and information regarding head injury in general and the elderly population in particular remain few and far between. Patients over the age of 60 are most likely to be treated as hopeless cases, with only a minimal chance of recovery, and even then expected to be left with such residual damage that they will no longer be able to function with any degree of independence.

EPIDEMIOLOGY

British mortality rates for 1991–2 are providing some useful information (OPCS). Table 5.1 gives data an accidental falls. For older people the majority of fatal falls occur at home (males: 334, females: 821), with the second commonest place being a communal establishment (males: 146, females: 455); steps and stairs are often involved. It is also notable that women are more prone to suffer from falls. Although these figures reflect mortality rates, it is obvious that head injury is a major cause of death as a result of such accidents. The interesting trend in lower death rates for falls since 1985 may suggest that there has been a change in the treatment of such cases and that survival rate may have improved. Unfortunately the figures do not delineate the type of injury resulting from falls.

Table 5.2 lists data for road traffic accidents. The differences between 1983 and 1991 in overall RTA figures for England and Wales do show an improvement, probably due to the introduction of the seat belt law. However, there has been an alarming increase in the death rate from RTAs for the older age group. When the cause of death is examined, skull,

Table 5.1 Accidental falls

	Males		Females	
	1985	1991	1985	1991
All ages	1430	1342	2477	2039
65–74	231	224	266	186
75+	723	655	2045	1697

Table 5.2 Road traffic accidents (OPCS, 1991–2)

	Males			Females		
	England & Wales		Scotland	England and Wales		Scotland
	1983	1991	1992	1983	1991	1992
All ages	4255	3071	319	1716	1337	144
15–44	2812	1865	203	812	470	40
45–64	490	460	48	280	212	26
65–74	132	245	26	143	199	17
75+	109	299	26	140	352	30

neck and trunk fractures, plus injuries to the chest, abdomen and pelvis appear to be the most common. This implies that head injury in the older age group is a growing matter of concern. It is puzzling as to why there has been such an increase in mortality for those over 65 years. Are more older people driving, are more confused people wandering about the streets, are there more problems of sight and hearing? There must be an explanation, and it would seem important to ascertain the reason if preventative measures are to be initiated.

The Scottish figures suggest that the main cause is a motor vehicle in collision with a pedestrian. There are a small number due to collisions with another vehicle, although it remains unclear as to whether the older person is the driver or a passenger.

It is also of interest to note that, until over the age of 75 years, men are more likely to suffer death from RTAs, but after 75 the mortality rate for women is the higher one. This could reflect the larger numbers of women surviving into extreme old age. Unfortunately the figures only give information regarding death from head injury and give no account of survivors or their condition.

In 1982 Jennett indicated that approximately one million head injury cases attended British casualty units each year, but only one in five were admitted – within 48 hours two thirds were discharged and about 5% were sent to a neurosurgical unit. He stated that in Scotland 830 per 100 000 patients over 65 years attended accident clinics in comparison to 1184 per 100 000 aged 25–64 years:

- admissions: 30% older group, 20% younger group;
- attending casualty: 6% over 64 years;
- admission from casualty: 9% elderly patients;
- coma 6+ hours: 11% elderly patients;
- fatalities: 25% over 64 years;
- neurosurgical interventions for intracranial haematomas: 13% over 64 years.

Road traffic accidents with older people usually involve them as pedestrians or passengers and the high rate of falls has a close association with alcohol consumption.

Fife (1986) examined the hospital admissions in Rhode Island and found that length of hospitalization increased with age, and hospital deaths or discharge to residential care increased 20 fold with increasing age. The longer the stay at any age the greater the likelihood of death or long term care. The national statistics in the USA, as in Great Britain, are not as informative as would be desirable. Fife (1987) suggests that the annual incidence of head injury in the USA is between 180 and 294 per 100 000, but points out that the figures are an underestimation as they are limited to very serious cases admitted to hospital or resulting in death. Those who were not admitted, but who still suffered after effects, were not included and thus the figures greatly underestimate the real problem. Estimates do seem to vary – another study (Ranseen, 1985) quotes 7 million head injuries resulting in 100 000 fatalities, 500 000 hospitalizations and 50 000 left with serious impairments. Yudofsky, Silver and Hales (1992) estimate over 2 million people in the USA suffer from traumatic brain injury each year (which seems an incredible drop in comparison with the 1985 figures), 500 000 are hospitalized and over 70 000 survivors are left with serious sequelae. This implies an annual incidence of 370 per 100 000 with brain injuries.

Jennett (1982) found that survival rates for those over 64 years was very low indeed. In a study with 134 patients over 64 years and in coma for over 6 hours only 5% regained independent living. He reported that if an older patient develops an acute intracranial haematoma benefit from surgery will occur as long as the coma is not deep and the person's physical condition is reasonably good. In such instances the recovery rate is about a quarter, but if the coma is deep and the physical state poor the prognosis is not good.

Further evidence of poor survival was offered by Finelli *et al.* (1989) in the USA who reported that mortality in the elderly group was nearly double that of the younger one (27% versus 14%). They also pointed out that the cost of care for older people was much higher than for the younger group and recommended earlier admission to a special unit in order to minimize risk and increase the person's chances of survival.

EFFECTS OF HEAD INJURY

Local injury

Wounds, lacerations, bruises or localized head injuries may look very unpleasant and appear serious, but open head injury is rarely as traumatic in the long run as the closed case, where there may be no external evidence whatsoever. Penetrating wounds due to falls, physical attacks or work accidents often only involve areas in the immediate vicinity of the wound; there is rarely a contre-coup effect (opposite poles) and fractured bones act as buffers. There may be a resultant limb weakness, a fit or other localized reaction, but loss of consciousness for longer than 5 minutes does not usually occur, if at all. As with any head injury, careful investigation and follow-up are necessary to ensure that more serious damage to the brain has not occurred. With increasing age, greater care and monitoring become essential.

Closed head injury

Loss of consciousness is of great importance in diagnosis, prognosis and treatment. A period of unconsciousness that exceeds 5 minutes in duration will almost certainly imply the existence of brain injury, some of which could be permanent. Even mild damage can lead to fatalities. Secondary events can develop after a patient has regained consciousness and apparently talked sensibly to staff and relatives. One third of head injury cases have suffered from a secondary infection or raised intracranial pressure. Vascular complications also play a major role in fatal outcome.

The effects of head injury depend on the direction of the blow, the force, the velocity and the freedom of movement of the head. The site of impact will have contusions and lacerations and there are also contra-coup effects. If the head is at rest the injuries will be at their maximum at the site of injury. If the head is in motion the contra-coup effects are usually worse.

Acceleration–deceleration injuries

These injuries are the result of movement, force and velocity related to impact. For instance, a motorcyclist may hit another vehicle, be flung into the air and crash into the vehicle, a wall or the ground. The brain may appear to be well protected, lying inside layers of bone, membrane and fluid, but it must be appreciated that it is still free to move about despite the protection. In the case of an unfortunate motorcyclist, the rate of movement and the force of impact would send the brain crashing about inside the skull. When the rate of movement is considerably accelerated the protective coverings are inadequate and the brain becomes vulnerable to, at least, bruising and, at worst, severe damage. In acceleration–deceleration situations swirling movements in the tissues result, these rotational and linear stresses tear up nerve fibres in any part of the brain and damage can be widespread.

Complications

Cerebral oedema This is swelling which occurs usually around the site of the lesion, and is quite common. As the lesions heal it will settle down, but it can be serious enough to cause infarcts or haematomas, which may prove fatal.

Vascular lesions Little haemorrhages can result from the shearing of nerve fibres and from general injuries. Large and small infarcts may occur and even arteries can become necrotic. Subdural haematomas, blood in the central nervous system and obstructions caused by blood – which leads to a hydrocephalus – are all possible complications of head injury.

Cerebral anoxia Lack of oxygen due to circulatory disorders, blood loss or breathing problems caused by chest injuries are further complications.

Acute stages of head injury

(1) Impairment of consciousness – from a moment to a prolonged coma.
(2) A variable period of confusion and awareness.
(3) A variable period of amnesia – post-traumatic amnesia (PTA) retrograde amnesia (RA).

These three stages usually follow on from each other during the course of recovery.

(1) Concussion This results from a blow to the head or impact with a blunt object. There is a consequent impairment of neuronal function. Loss of consciousness is the obvious feature of this stage. Mild confusion may not indicate permanent effects on the brain, but it is now generally accepted that loss of consciousness for over 5 minutes implies that some form of permanent damage will ensue. It is also recognized that repeated injury to the head, even when there are long intervals between, can cause permanent damage.

It can be argued that boxers and other sports people can suffer concussion without losing consciousness. A series of blows to the head, a bad fall or a collision with another player can induce confused thought processes and lethargy over varying periods of time. A boxer who regularily engages in fights can become 'punch drunk', each damaging bout adding even more injury to that already sustained. Cumulative effects can be as serious as instant ones – encephalitis pugilistica being one possible outcome.

Minor accidents, such as those in sports, should be treated with caution as delayed effects can occur. The classic example is that of the footballer who, after a collision, loses consciousness for a few seconds, recovers and continues to play – yet later has no recall for any of the events following the collision. Other side effects such as slurred or confused speech, disorders of perception or movement can appear some time after the incident, and can reappear from time to time later on.

(2) Variable period of awareness The period between trauma and return to full consciousness and awareness of day to day events can take many forms from apparently psychotic behaviour to apathy and withdrawal. It is sometimes referred to as the psychiatric phase. The person may be manic and the staff are in despair as he or she makes demands, disrupts routines, interferes with others and cannot stay still. Paranoia is possible. The patient may insist that the doctor or nurse was responsible for the injuries, and may even become violent. Confabulation, delusions or hallucinations are common, thinking is impaired and the person is disorientated for a time, place and person. On the other hand the person may appear quite sensible most of the time and staff and relatives believe that he or she has returned to normal.

This period can prove severe and extended for elderly people. It may persist for months and observers may conclude that a dementia is present. A poor physical state, a history of alcoholism or vascular disorders can exacerbate the situation.

(3) Particular amnesic effects (a) PTA plays an important role when the degree of severity of an injury and the prognosis are being judged: PTA refers to the period of time from the moment of the accident and loss of consciousness to the time when the person becomes continuously aware of events around him or her and is capable, once again, of remembering day to day happenings. As apparent clarity of thought and speech can occur during PTA it is often difficult to be sure when PTA is over. Patients can usually confirm this themselves.

Some of the periods of lucidity can be recalled later, but generally the entire period from the accident has not been stored in a retrieveable manner and that time and the events have been completely lost. The length of PTA is very important, as the longer it is the more severe the brain damage. The accepted rule is:

0–5 minutes	mild concussion
less than an hour	mild deficits
1–24 hours	moderate deficits
1–7 days	severe deficits
more than 7 days	very severe deficits

The length of PTA has implications for the ability to return to work (Steadman and Graham, 1970):

PTA less than an hour	1 month
PTA less than a day	2 months
PTA less than a week	4 months
PTA more than a week	at least a year, if at all

A study by Brooks *et al.* (1987) followed 134 severely head injured patients of differing ages over 7 years and found that of the 85% of those who were working prior to injury 71% were no longer working after injury. Their findings with regard to the length of PTA were in agreement with previous studies – the longer the PTA the less likely a return to work. Brooks *et al.* also found that age was a major factor in recovery and agreed with the opinions of many writers including Humphrey and Oddy (1980) who considered age to be a critical factor, finding that with age a patient's adaptability was reduced and that employers were unwilling to take on older workers with reduced ability or possible impairments.

Studies are also suggesting a link with social recovery, and with the development of psychiatric sequelae. Memory may remain unsteady even with apparent recovery by older people after a lengthy PTA.

(b) RA is the time between the moment of injury and loss of consciousness to the last clear, continuous memory *before* the accident. This is usually much shorter than the PTA, but not always so. Normally it is only for a few minutes, and the person can remember leaving home and several other events prior to the accident. Mild cases may have no RA at all; in serious cases RA may encompass days, weeks or even months. Often as the patient recovers the RA period becomes shorter and shorter as more memories return. Sometimes the RA actually lengthens. It is extremely rare for a patient with anything more than a moderate concussion to remember the actual accident.

Unusually long RAs are sometimes thought to be psychogenic, but there is evidence that they can be organic too. There has been very little research on the nature of RA and it would be interesting to know how often elderly people suffer from an extended RA in comparison with younger patients. PTA and RA have been rather loosely left to the injured person's judgement – usually quite satisfactorily. The Galveston

Orientation and Amnesia Test (GOAT) developed by Levin, O'Donnell and Grossman (1979) can be used as a more objective measure of both PTA and RA periods. More detailed accounts of head injury, its diagnosis, prognosis and treatment can be found in textbooks such as by Brooks (1984) and Garner (1990).

Other complications

It is important not to miss evidence of fracture, epilepsy, meningitis or haematoma. About 5%, or approximately 5000 patients, a year will have a fit within a week of sustaining a head injury. This may prove a problem in the future as epileptic fits can recur up to 4 years later. The degree and risk of epilepsy can now be estimated fairly accurately.

Even after consciousness and awareness have been regained brain damage can be so severe as to cause permanent damage to abilities and daily living skills. Handicaps are often physical – broken bones which fail to recover full mobility, disfiguring scars etc., but there are also permanent or persistent impairments to brain function. During at least the following two years post-trauma, improvements occur, but changes in work and social outlets will probably result. Aphasias and physical disabilities are expected, but other more subtle changes can cause friction at home, at work and socially. The effects on memory, personality and intellectual ability are harder to accept or understand.

Many patients over 65 years of age develop a chronic subdural haematoma and this is frequently overlooked as there may be no record of a head injury. Its identification depends on general practitioners, geriatricians and psychiatrists who have noticed the presence of persistent headaches and slight weakness or paralysis. The patient will probably show evidence of recent deterioration in intellectual abilities. Surgical interventions are usually quite successful. On the other hand, acute intracranial haematomas which occur within the first few days or weeks post trauma are less promising prognostically with older people.

ASSESSMENT PROCEDURES

Assessment of the degree and severity of head injury covers a wide range of procedures. Obviously scans, radiography and laboratory investigations are of particular importance. Here more observational methods will be considered. The scale in most common use is probably the Glasgow Coma Scale (Teasdale and Jennett, 1974). This simple instrument concentrates on the opening of eyes and the quality of verbal and motor responses. Staff can monitor reactions during the first few hours and days after injury, and by carefully recording response or lack of response, can judge changes in the patient's conscious condition.

The Glasgow Outcome Scale (Jennett and Bond, 1975) has five categories, which simply state degrees of disablement from permanent vegetative state to full recovery. It is used over a period of 6 months as a guide to progress and prognosis.

The GOAT mentioned above, Levin *et al.* 1979) is useful in measuring PTA and RA.

The Rancho Los Amigos scale of cognitive levels and expected behaviour (Hagen and Malkmus, 1979) looks at behavioural stages in the progress of recovery and concentrates on the highest level of cognitive functioning that is present throughout the recovery period.

The Disability Rating Scale (Rappaport *et al.*, 1982) was introduced to detect and measure clinical changes in individuals who had sustained severe head injury. It was felt that the Glasgow Outcome Scale was not sufficiently sensitive and a guide to those most likely to respond to rehabilitation was necessary. A study examining the reliability and validity of this test justified its use in monitoring recovery (Gouvier *et al.*, 1987).

Once the patient is fully aware of events and surroundings and the PTA has been estimated, neuropsychological investigations can be initiated. Obviously it will be necessary to use these in accord with the individual's ability to respond or to concentrate. The elderly in particular will require gentle approaches (refer to Chapter 2).

Laterality is a factor to consider when assessing older people. Just because he or she appears to be right handed, or because right handedness is assumed, it does not follow that the person is left hemisphere dominant. Until more recent years left handed children were persuaded, or even forced, to write with the traditional right hand. Left handedness was regarded as socially unacceptable or something to joke about, so teachers, and often parents, stressed the 'proper' use of the right hand. This enforced change can lead to problems and errors in assessment and location of damage. A right handed patient might have brain damage which is overlooked because there is no language disorder. Equally a person who can write with the left hand may have language impairments, instead of perceptual or spatial difficulties, which may be missed. If the person is unable to communicate, he or she cannot explain the ambidexterity. Without careful questioning and close observation the 'crossed' laterality could lead to errors in the identification of impairments and limit the degree of useful assistance available to the patient.

OTHER RESEARCH FINDINGS

Although improvements have occurred in the amount of attention that has been attributed to head injury in recent years, the older patient still appears in most studies almost as an after thought. Delayed response and slow recovery as well as memory impairents are consistently reported.

Miller (1984) examined the available studies carefully and questioned the assumption that it was possible to compare the damage caused to older brains with those of younger ones. It is well nigh impossible to find perfectly matched lesions, furthermore pre-existing experience and behavioural patterns will be different. In children verbal material will still be recently acquired, so if the left hemisphere is damaged it will be easier for the right hemisphere to take over, whereas in adults with an established language system a lesion in the left hemisphere will almost certainly have a different outcome. Past experience and personality, depending on the individual, can help or hinder recovery. Older people may have had some pretraumatic disease process in operation which may become obvious after trauma. **It is important to stress the simple fact – everyone is different.**

Each human being is not only distinct in external looks, but will be probably unique internally too, including the brain. Two people may be suffering from an agnosia for example, but symptoms, strengths and coping skills will be very different. Each person will call upon previous experience, personality, intelligence and acquired knowledge. The outcome for those two people will differ according to the way they use their resources. These are some of the reasons why it is so difficult to study deficits. It is almost, if not entirely, impossible to match subjects in examining rehabilitation strategies or even in furthering understanding of brain damage.

External factors can make a difference to recovery too. Attitudes of staff and relatives who have digested the widely held belief that older people have a poor prognosis for recovery, may not provide the attention or seek to remotivate as adroitly as with younger patients. Other factors such as the fallacious adage 'you can't teach an old dog new tricks' may influence the reactions of others and lead to lack of confidence in applying any attempt at rehabilitation. The general acceptance of such myths has lead employers to hesitate before employing older workers, so re-employment of an older person post-traumatically becomes even more unlikely.

Recently several British companies have used a retraining programme for their employees when there was a change in the type of production. It was found that the older ones adapted extremely well, using previous skills to add to the new ones. They had no difficulty in learning the new methods, were more conscientious than younger employees and were found to be very reliable and enthusiastic.

It is to be hoped that such a venture is put to use more frequently and the implications for those recovering from head injury appreciated as well.

A study by Wilson *et al.* (1987) provided a 6 month follow-up of 54 head injury patients over 65 years (average age 77.2 years). All five with severe and three with moderate injury died. Amongst the survivors post-trauma headaches were a common feature; memory and concentration were causing problems with 10 people 1–6 weeks later; 43% were less mobile than previously 6 weeks later. The older group (mean age 83.4 years) had problems with activities of daily living and also required much more service support than the younger group (mean age 76.1 years), who maintained their independence.

This study also confirmed previous findings implicating alcohol as a contributory factor to head injury in two thirds of the male patients. The authors stress that lack of confidence in the older patients was probably the main reason for the fall in self care and strongly recommended the need for a plan of support and early intervention so that rehabilitation could prove more effective.

A series of studies from Scotland (Andrews *et al.*, 1990; Gentleman and Jennett, 1990; Gentleman, Jennett and MacMillan, 1992) all stress the importance of getting head injury patients to a neurosurgical unit as soon as possible in order to provide the best available service to save life and maintain quality of living on discharge. A similar call for early intervention and care in the USA has been made by Finelli *et al.* (1989).

Andrews *et al.* (1990) and Gentleman and Jennett (1990) note the possible added trauma that might occur during transport and offer advice on measures to employ before transfer. Although there are potential dangers in transporting such patients all writers express a belief that more lives can be saved with such admissions. Gentleman *et al.* (1992) reported that although many of the untransferred elderly patients died from irremediable causes, others, who were too seriously injured to be transferred to a special unit, could be saved with better communication between general hospitals and the staff at neurosurgical units. If transfer was deemed too dangerous, discussion and co-operation between specialties would assist. The patient population in the 1992 study (Gentleman *et al.*) averaged 72 years (range 2 months to 101 years); RTAs accounted for 49% and falls for 44%.

An interesting investigation by Tellier *et al.* (1990) of Second World War veterans, all of whom had suffered from severe penetrating skull wounds and had post traumatic epilepsy, found that they were living more or less normal lives 40 years later – only two were in residential homes. Surprisingly, although they had recovered to a remarkable degree, those with right anterior damage were showing greater maladjustment to all dimensions of life than those with left anterior damage.

THE PROCESS OF RECOVERY

Restoration of function is a most complex activity and the reasons why it occurs remain unclear. Various theories have been offered, and continue to be offered, but the process is still an unsolved mystery. Improvements do occur, sometimes function returns to normal or near normal and on other occasions improvement is minimal. The details of the theories regarding restoration of brain function will only be mentioned briefly here, but the reader can consult various books such as those by Texler (1987) or Muir Giles and Clark-Wilson (1993) for more information.

One theory was von Monakow's **diaschsis**, which implied that there was an inhibitory effect, arising from the lesion, which spread to distant parts of the brain connected to the lesion by fibre pathways – a more or less temporary shock from which the affected areas recovered in due course.

Another possibile explanation was offered by Luria: **inhibition**. He believed that a lesion could stun or disrupt the activity in other parts of the brain, perhaps by interference in neurotransmitter production. The involvement or takeover by **secondary systems** is another theory – when the original system has been damaged, underlying systems take its place until either the original one recovers or the parts that are spared can operate effectively.

Reorganization implies that another system altogether can become responsible for a damaged function. **Functional adaptation** refers to the way a person with brain damage learns to use other mechanisms than those previously employed to achieve his or her intentions, complete a task or perform an action.

Craine (1987) decries the pessimism surrounding rehabilitation programmes which concentrate on compensating for lost function, and offers more positive avenues of approach which could be applied to elderly patients as well as more youthful ones. He and his colleagues have devised a retraining programme which they call **neurotraining**, the principles of which will be outlined in Chapter 6. Although he describes some of the theories, his main influence is that of Luria (1963, 1969) who believed that restoration could not succeed without specific rehabilitative therapy. Craine accepts that natural recovery does take place over the subsequent 18 months to 2 years, but during that time, and afterwards, support and retraining systems are necessary in order to ensure optimum improvement. Whatever the reasons for restoration of function, it would seem logical to provide nature with help – a precious garden plant knocked down by rain or wind will grow again, but without the assistance of a stake it will develop unsightly bends and curves; man and his brain are much more complex, but surely even more deserving of assistance.

HEAD INJURY, BRAIN DAMAGE AND ELDERLY PEOPLE

It is plain from the recent figures that there is an increase in the number of older people suffering from head injury, be the accidents due to falls, RTAs or whatever. There is a general outcry and protest from head injury services about the poor attention and minimal support they receive (e.g. Pentland and Miller, 1988). It is almost impossible for a head injured patient to be admitted to a suitable rehabilitation unit – they are mostly private, cost too much for local authorities and are situated away from the patient's area. The fact that the person may well become independent and capable of self support with appropriate retraining appears to be irrelevant, as is the fact that without structured rehabilitation the person will in due course cost the local authority even more in time because of an increasing level of dependency. Short sighted policies reap their own reward, unfortunately they have dire effects on the innocent members of the community.

Community care is proving far from satisfactory for many confused elderly patients and in many instances untrained staff are desperately trying to cope with problems encountered in the homes of their clients. There is insufficient advice, recommendations or ideas available in many areas with the result that treatment or management programmes are limited or completely omitted. It is tragic that trained staff are so stretched and limited in number, but it is of equal concern that those who have sustained head injury are deprived of appropriate services to the extent that they are.

The fate of older head injured people is disastrous. The myths surrounding ageing are pejorative enough, but add a head injury to the situation and the response becomes even more dismissive. The studies of the past, which included one or two over 65s, consistantly concluded that there was a poor prognosis for the older subjects. More recent articles stress the need to prevent death by early intervention, but the old attitude persists. If the older patients do not die, they can be left with such damage that they become permanent members of a continuing care ward. Staff, and sometimes relatives, who believe that 'nothing can be done' may continue the outmoded pattern of leaving the person alone. So alone that there is no information, reassurance, encouragement or attempts to introduce positive approaches to care. As in the case of post-operative confusion proper assessment, appropriate interventions and modified environments are not always considered. Sadly there is little evidence to show any change in attitudes. There is no evidence of studies examining what could happen if a more active rehabiitation programme was introduced. If the older patient makes a recovery of sorts, either he or she is admitted to a continuing care ward – today it would be a residential home – or sent home to the care of relatives or home care staff, despite their lack of knowledge regarding the best approaches to employ.

There has been no attempt to evaluate the effects of the environment, both physical and psychological. Psychological factors may play a major role in the recovery of older patients (Miller, 1984). Younger people have a family who are usually anxious to understand and help, the older person may live alone, lack loving support and have nothing worthwhile to which to return. The prospect of coping with daily living and self care in a disabled state can severely affect motivation and the will to live. It is not unusual to hear a 70–80 year old state 'What is there to live for? I cannot care for myself properly, I have nothing to offer and no one who cares – what's the point?'. Survival in a lonely, uncaring world is not conducive to effort. The alternative to living and coping alone is residential care. The choice is not pleasant and the future not one to be eagerly embraced by any other than those who actively enjoy being 'ill'. However, most individuals do wish to continue to live, even those who have doubts, and if they are provided with more attention, rehabilitation and social outlets their motivation could be fed. Unfortunately, in the present climate such a service is very difficult to find.

There is a crying need for more training, more rehabilitation units and better understanding of the methods that could be used to help older people as well as the younger head injured. There should be better appreciation of environmental influences, psychological needs and strategies of rehabilitation geared especially for the later years. Staff training should assist in minimizing the negative attitudes towards care; neurosurgical ward staff should be aware of the special needs of older people and of the possible approaches that could be used to assist recovery and independence and authorities should make more effort to provide services for those with head injury.

TWO CASE REPORTS

A brief account of two older people where head injury was suspected might serve to demonstrate how easy it is for staff or the general public to make assumptions on the basis of observed behaviour and a lack of careful investigations.

Case 1

Mr S was admitted on to a general hospital ward after falling in the street and losing consciousness. His confusion apparently lasted for some time and three days later the staff reported that he continued to be confused, disorientated and apparently deteriorating mentally. As he had been drinking prior to the fall it was suspected that he might be an alcoholic. Radiography had failed to locate a fracture, so a scan was booked and a neuropsychologist was asked for an opinion.

Mr S was in his 70s, lived alone and had been active and independent with a good circle of friends. In his present condition the staff were concerned about his ability to maintain his previous independence. After a general discussion with the neuropsychologist Mr S explained that he could not remember exactly what happened to him. He suspected that he had 'one too many' when he went for his regular Sunday visit to the pub. When asked simple questions relating to time and place he replied that he had no idea. When gently pressed to supply more information he said 'If you look out of the windows here what can you see? Nothing but blank walls. There is no clock, no newspaper and no one to talk to. I was "out cold" when I came in here and I don't know how long that lasted. No one has told me a thing and I have no means of finding out the answers to any of your questions'.

When told the name of the hospital he accurately described its whereabouts. He was informed of the length of his stay and told the day and date. The following day he had no difficulty in responding correctly to any orientation questions recalling the events around his admission as outlined the previous day, and his general response was normal. No evidence was found to support the assumption that he was other than naturally confused after his fall. Within a couple of days he was discharged home perfectly fit and able.

The problem here lay with an unhelpful environment and with staff assumptions, rather than with the patient or his injuries. Simple common sense and a more informative environment would have avoided unnecessary stress for Mr S and the queries would never have arisen.

Case 2

Miss K, aged 87 years, had been knocked down by a car 6 months prior to neuropsychological investigations. She had sustained some physical injuries and walked with a slight limp. Her lawyer was seeking compensation for injury, but felt that at such an age any mental disability would be regarded as due to 'senility' and it would be impossible to differentiate between this and possible brain damage in a way that would convince a court of law.

Miss K had been a student of Carl Jung, eventually specializing in the treatment of childhood disorders. Until two years previously she had clinical input with asthma patients and was now considering reopening another treatment centre. She felt that this might be a little unrealistic in view of her age! On examination it was quickly established that she was of very superior intelligence and a highly cultured woman. Although rather garrulous, her performance on neuropsychological and other tests was incredibly fast and almost perfect.

Three months before her accident, when she was 86 years old, she had been in Denmark where she travelled about the country on a hired moped! This remarkable woman had no knowledge of the Danish language but found no problem in interpreting the international road signs. Three months prior to the accident she had been perfectly capable of understanding and using visual material, 6 months after the accident she had great difficulty in interpreting any material of a similar nature!

The court awarded damages which made the remaining years of her life, spent in a private, comfortable residential home, exceedingly pleasant.

It was assumed that age alone would cause deterioration, that the notion of 'senility' could be applied and that it would be impossible to detect damage caused by external events. The case of Miss K can also demonstrate the danger of assuming that with age a person's intelligence disintegrates. An older intelligent person may lose a little of his or her ability, but can remain more able than many of those in a caring or professional role!

SUGGESTIONS REGARDING THE REHABILITATION OF ELDERLY HEAD INJURED PATIENTS

It is, of course, vital that appropriate investigations and treatment for head injury should be instigated as soon as possible, but there are other factors to be considered when a patient is over 65 years. The basic format for all head injury cases of any age is, obviously, relevant to the older group too, and the protocol is:

Initially:

- medical and neurological investigations, including scans and laboratory tests;
- use of relevant assessments of function – Glasgow Coma Scale;
- collection of relevant information regarding social background, physical and psychological history, possible intellectual level, routines;
- consistant observation.

After initial care:

- team discussion regarding treatment and management programmes to be commenced as soon as possible;
- environmental influences to be controlled – lighting, familiar faces and things, lack of isolation, low noise level, limit to change or moves, limit to interference to sleep;
- continued monitoring and recording – Glasgow Outcome Scale, Rancho Los Amigos, etc.;

- goal setting graded to meet individual's ability;
- involvement of other support/therapy staff – OTs, physiotherapists, speech therapists, psychologists, etc.;
- careful thought to be given to ways in which to motivate, reassure and encourage the patient;
- once it is possible to obtain some co-operation and the attention span has improved, look for specific retained and damaged functions using appropriate tests, e.g. neuropsychological investigations;
- a meaningful support system must be set up for discharge purposes.

In the early stages of recovery, attention is transient, the person may still have a PTA so awareness is only vague and information will not be stored. However, that does not mean that it is unnecessary to provide some input. A person in a confused state does require some structure in a world that seems unreal. Staff and relatives can be of considerable assistance by helping to restore a patient's body image. Each contact with the person fighting to regain consciousness is an opportunity to assist. Personal identity can be re-established by taking the person's hand and putting it to his or her forehead and saying something such as 'Do you feel hot and sticky? There, can you feel if your forehead is hot?' and then 'Would you like to wash your face? Here's a face cloth, you take it, now you try to wipe your face, it might make you feel better'. A guiding hand can help the patient to reassociate sensation with self awareness.

A simple form of reality orientation can be of use at this early stage too (Corrigan *et al.*, 1985; Holden and Woods, 1988). The use of cards from family and friends, discovering particular interests and bringing in objects related to these to discuss or comment on, or even listening to favourite types of music, are all ways to encourage recognition and the use of memory, skills and knowledge. Well engrained information and behavioural responses are tools to be employed in rehabilitation.

Early and regular contact is of importance as it helps a person to realize that someone cares. This is so important to a lonely old person that it cannot be stressed enough. The patient needs a reason to fight, to recover and to continue living, constructive time spent in reawakening a sense of worth and a will to live will build up motivation. Older patients require warmth and prompting to a greater degree otherwise deterioration or at least a longer hospitalization will prove inevitable.

Once the person is more aware of events proper assessment will provide clues to the areas of retained ability and damage to be used in rehabilitative programmes. When these become apparent, more structured retraining is necessary and should be initiated as soon as the person is physically and emotionally ready. If the process of establishing good relationships and an encouraging atmosphere have been in operation since the first signs of minimal awareness then such programmes can develop smoothly and easily. The chances of a satisfactory outcome will be greater and will provide more opportunity to evaluate the widely accepted belief that older people have a poorer prognosis post-trauma than younger ones.

With people over 65 years the concern does not end with a fairly good restoration of awareness, there remains the problem of return home. Even if a person has a continuing disability and requires residential care, plans do not end on discharge. To allow a head injured elderly person back into the community without making arrangements to ensure his or her safety, continued recovery and peace of mind is to guarantee that all the good work will soon be undone. The person will become depressed, withdrawn, lose confidence or deteriorate quickly unless there is a good support system. To leave the standard of living of such a patient in the hands of untrained and uninformed staff can only amount to a death sentence.

After considering discharge plans at a team meeting it is advisable to:

(1) Discuss the situation with the patient and spouse or relatives, if there are any. Stress the need to treat the patient as a person and not a total invalid. Explain what can be done and what needs to be done.
(2) Call on the help of a community psychiatric nurse (CPN) in order to monitor progress and advise on difficulties.
(3) Hopefully there has been team involvement, in which case individual team members will want to reassess progress too.
(4) If the person is alone at home, then a team approach for support should be instigated.
(5) If the person is discharged into a residential setting, then careful explanations, advice and relevant programmes should be discussed with the staff and arrangements made to monitor progress.

It is imperative that all concerned fully appreciate the strengths, needs and emotions involved.

It is vital to appreciate that head injury is not a subject understood by those who have had little or no contact with trauma. Mistakes and misunderstandings can arise and, if they do, then the patient's welfare is in jeopardy. Furthermore, relatives are liable to suffer and become very stressed. They too need support, but understanding can make a major difference to attitudes and often calms a potentially catastrophic situation.

REFERENCES

Andrews, P.J.D., Piper, I.R., Dearden, N.M. and Miller, J.D. (1990) Secondary insults during intrahospital transport of head injured patients. *The Lancet*, **335**, 327–30.

Brooks, D.N. (1984) *Closed Head Injury: Psychological, Social and Family Consequences*, Oxford University Press, Oxford.

Brooks, N., Mckinley, W. Symington, C., *et al.* (1987) Return to work within the first seven years of severe head injury. *Brain Injury*, **1**, No. 1, 5–19.

Corrigan, J.D., Arnett, J.A., Houck, L.J. and Jackson, R.D. (1985) Reality orientation for brain injured patients: group treatment and monitoring of recovery. *Archives of Physical Medicine and Rehabilitation*, **66**, 626–39.

Craine, J.F. (1987) Principles of cognitive rehabilitation, *Cognitive Rehabilitation*, (ed. L.E. Texler), Plenum Press, New York.

Fife, D. (1986) Incidence and outcome of hospital treated head injury in Rhode Island. *American Journal of Public Health*, **76**, 773–8.

Fife, D. (1987) Head injury with and without hospital admission: comparisons of incidence and short-term disablity. *American Journal of Public Health*, **77**, 810–12.

Finelli, F.C., Jonsson, J., Champion, H.R., *et al.* (1989) A case control study for major trauma in geriatric patients. *The Journal of Trauma*, **29**(5), 541–8.

Garner, R. (1990) *Acute Head Injury*, Chapman & Hall, London.

Gentleman, D. and Jennett, B. (1990) Audit of transfer of unconscious head injured patients to a neurosurgical unit. *The Lancet*, **335**, 330–4.

Gentleman, D., Jennett, B. and MacMillan, R. (1992) Death in hospital after head injury without transfer to a neurosurgical unit: who, when and why? *Injury: The British Journal of Accident Surgery*, **23**(7), 471–4.

Gouvier, W.D., Blanton, P.D., LaPorte, K.K. and Nepomuceno, C. (1987) Reliability and validity of the disability rating scale and the levels of cognitive functioning in monitoring recovery from severe head injury. *Archives Physical Medicine Rehabilitation*, **68**, 94–7.

Hagen, C. and Malkmus, D. (1979) (The Rancho Los Amigos Scale) Intervention strategies for language disorders secondary to head traua. *American Speech–Language Hearing Association Short courses*, Atlanta.

Holden, U.P. and Woods, R.T. (1988) *Reality Orientation: Psychological Approaches to the 'Confused' Elderly*, 2nd edn, Churchill Livingstone, Edinburgh and New York.

Humphrey, M. and Oddy, M. (1980) Return to work after head injury: a review of post war studies. *Injury*, **12**, 107–14.

Jennett, B. (1982) Head injury in the elderly, *Neurosurgical Disorders in the Elderly*, (ed. F.J. Caird), Wright, Bristol.

Jennett, B. and Bond, M.R. (1975) Assessment of outcome after severe brain injury. *Lancet*, **i**, 480–4.

Levin, H.S., O'Donnell, V.M. and Grossman, R.G. (1979) The Galveston Orientation and Amnesia Test: a practical scale to assess cognition after head injury. *Journal of Nervous and Mental Disease*, **167**, 675–84.

Luria, A.R. (1963) *Restoration of Function after Brain Injury*, McMillan, Oxford.

Luria, A.R., Naydin, V.L., Tsvetkova, L.S. and Vinarskaya, E.N. (1969) Restoration of higher cortical function following local brain damage, in *Handbook of Clinical Neurology*, Vol. 3, (eds R.S. Vinken and G.W. Bruyn), North Holland, Amsterdam.

Miller, E. (1984) *Recovery and Management of Neuropsychological Impairments*, Wiley, Chichester and New York.

Muir Giles, G. and Clarke-Wilson, J. (1993) *Brain Injury Rehabilitation*, Chapman Hall, London. Office of Population Censuses and Surveys (1991–4) *Mortality Rates In England and Wales*.

Pentland, B. and Miller, D. (1988) Head injury rehabilitation: 4 years experience in Edinburgh. *British Journal of Neurology*, **2**, 61–5.

Ranseen, J.D. (1985) Comprehensive rehabilitation of head injured adults. *MMJ*, **34**(12), 1176–82.

Rappaport, M., Hall, K.M., Hopkins, E. and Belleza, T. (1982) Disability Rating

Scale for severe head trauma: coma to community. *Archives Physical Medicine Rehabilitation*, **83**, 118–23.

Steadman, J.J. and Graham, J.G. (1970) Head injuries: an analysis and follow up study. *Proceedings of the Royal Society of Medicine*, **6**(3), 23–8.

Teasdale, G. and Jennett, B. (1974) Assessment of coma and impaired consciousness; a practical scale (Glasgow Coma Scale). *Lancet*, **ii**, 81–4.

Tellier, A., Walker, A.E., Adams, K.M. and Rourke, B.P. (1990) Long term effects of severe penetrating head injury on psychosocial adjustments. *Journal of Consulting Clinical Psychology*, **58**, 531–7.

Texler, L.E. (ed.) (1987). *Cognitive Rehabilitation*, Plenum Press, New York.

Wilson, J.A., Pentland, B., Currie, C.T. and Miller, J.D. (1987) Head injury in the elderly. *Brain Injury*, **1**(2), 183–8.

Yudofsky, S.C., Silver, J. and Hales, R.E. (1992) Neuropsychiatry of brain injury. *Current Opinion in Psychiatry*, **5**, 103–8.

Management, rehabilitation and retraining

> There are well established principles and strategies that can be incorporated into our programmes ... positive reinforcement, extinction, shaping ... teaching techniques from mental handicap, reality orientation from geriatrics ... and the individual approach from neuropsychology.
>
> *Wilson, 1981*

CRITICAL ISSUES

The role of a neuropsychologist was originally limited to assessment of damage and the search for explanations regarding impairments of function. It became increasingly obvious that simply to identify a problem was unsatisfactory and methods to actively help an affected person were of the greatest importance. Today it is the responsibility of a neuropsychologist to identify the problem, find retained strengths and abilities, develop retraining and rehabilitation programmes, evaluate them and provide evidence to show their effectiveness. However, the number of successful interventions that have been published remains disappointing (Miller, 1984; Miller and Morris, 1993).

One of the main reasons for the paucity of 'proven' methods is the fact that it is almost impossible to devise a programme that will serve to rehabilitate a large number of patients. Each person may be said to suffer from a similar deficit or impairment, but when closely observed it will soon become apparent that there are individual differences. For instance two people may suffer from agnosia, but when tested on a variety of tasks they will display different responses and use different ways to perform tasks or solve problems. This may be due to slightly different parts of the brain being involved or damaged, but it could also be due to differing backgrounds in experience, knowledge, expertise, culture and intelligence. An approach which might prove successful for one person may prove totally useless for another, so to develop a 'package' which could be applied to a group of people apparently suffering from the same impairments will not necessarily prove successful. Effective interventions can only be truly judged on a single case success story – if a person responds to a particular intervention and improves, then that programme has been appropriate for that particular person.

The lack of practical ideas available in print for rehabilitation or management guidelines does not mean that there are none available, or that there is no structured technique in use by therapists. There are a number to choose from, but individual needs must always be the main influence in deciding the most appropriate approach and specific method.

Physiotherapists, occupational therapist and speech therapists all use special techniques and methods in their daily work. However, there is a tendency for different disciplines to work in isolation from each other and there can be a reluctance, or some difficulty, in developing a team system where the differing approaches can be slotted together into a more effective whole.

Goal setting is an important part of any rehabilitation programme, but unfortunately it is often very loose and poorly organized. The nursing process is well recognized, but not always well practised. The targets may be stated in a negative manner: 'John Green must stop swearing', or set at an impossible level: 'Mary Parker will learn to speak properly'. Unfortunately poor Mary's stroke has left her with considerable damage to the speech system and she will never regain her previous ability to communicate with ease, and John's bad language may be in response to frustrating problems in his environment or the attitude of others.

In order to set goals and appropriate steps to recovery, a **multi-disciplinary team** is vital. Different disciplines can pool their information about the patient's strengths and weaknesses and reach agreement about priorities, staged interventions and consistent approaches. An awareness of the contribution of other team members limits unnecessary overlap or even contradiction. A parallel approach also lessens the confusion for the client by minimizing the number of different instructions and the multiplicity of strange faces.

Common sense in management is often neglected. Failing to recognize the feelings and fears of both client and family will lead to further complications, poor expectations and unwanted stress. It will also give rise to problems in co-operation. It cannot be stressed too strongly, the focus must be on the individual – his or her needs, interests, abilities, feelings, fears, experience and lifestyle, as such information is the basis of appropriate interventions, as well as providing an insight into the nature of the person's problems.

PRINCIPLES OF RESTORATION

Rehabilitation techniques are in their early stages and few can be traced back to pre 1940. Reality orientation was the first positive approach for older people and that was introduced in the late 1950s. Other interventions such as reminiscence, memory groups, movement to music, Kitwood's approach regarding social influences, or 'malignant social psychology' (Kitwood, 1993) and so forth are more recent (Holden and Woods, 1995), but none of them fully address neuropsychological deficits apart from memory problems. Most of the neuropsychological rehabilitation programmes have focused on head injury and on younger people (Trexler, 1987; Muir Giles and Clark-Wilson, 1993) though, with some necessary modifications, these programmes can work as well for older people and for those with degenerative conditions.

The theories regarding the recovery process are many in number and none of them have been proved, but the work of many researchers demonstrates that function can be restored and recovery or adaptation is possible. Craine (1987) offers eight principles, or guidelines, for restoring function which can be applied to elderly patients with some modifications:

(1) Recovery of function following cortical damage is possible. This positive attitude is essential for those working with any patients of whatever age. It encompasses several of the theories: another part of the brain can take over, either as an additional responsibility or because it is capable of several functions and has been held in reserve; the damage was temporary, rather like bruising, and will return in due course, or recovery is due to reorganisation through retraining. Luria *et al.* (1969) stated '. . . recovery of the function must not be attributed to transfer of the function to a new, vicarious centre but rather to a structural reorganization'.

It must also be recognized that nature can heal as well; spontaneous recovery can occur even after 2 years. A little support and direction can make this occur more effectively and possibly quicker.

Older people will need more encouragement and more support in order to avoid depression and poor motivation.

(2) The brain is an adaptive mechanism which can be halted or slowed by injury or environmental deprivation, or it can be made more active by stimulation. The theory here is that as the brain is responsible for learning an individual can make changes in response to external influences. So if the environment is encouraging and stimulating in a structured manner the person is given the opportunity to perceive this and respond. This places stress on providing a suitable environment for a patient, but it must be remembered that staff and relatives are part of that environment and their attitudes will play a role in recovery as well.

(3) In order to retain information repetition is essential. In learning any new skill there is a period of mistakes, forgetting and uncertainty. A learner driver is someone everyone treats with caution for obvious reasons. Eventually driving skills become automatic, as is the case with all skills. A child falls over innumerable times before walking steadily and it is only if a person has suffered from a broken leg that there is ever a further need to think carefully about how to make legs work. A person with specific damage to a function may well think that he or she can still use that function. It is necessary to return to stage one and relearn the whole process once again. The only way this can be achieved is by regular practice and concentration.

In any retraining programme, for any age, the need to succeed is paramount or the person will lose heart. This is particularily vital with older people. Whatever the task provided for practice, it must be set at the right level or failure will follow. Step by careful step is the rule. The starting point should be with a task that the therapist knows the person can do easily. Obviously this implies an appropriate assessment in order to find the base rate and the point where difficulties begin.

(4) As stated before, when a function has been damaged any automatic use will not be possible, so relearning must return to basic steps. It is essential that each step must be perfectly performed or grasped before moving on to the next step in order to avoid future difficulties.

(5) Awareness of sensory strengths and deficits. Once again assessment is vital to identify sensory areas which are retained or damaged. It will be useless to attempt retraining using visual material if the person has agnosia or other visual deficits; it is equally important to look at the other senses for the same reason. It is rare to find more than one or two senses in difficulty and the functioning ones will be the main basis for retraining purposes. Pairing the good sense with the damaged one will allow the weaker one to improve. For example a person may not recognize objects on a picture but his or her verbal ability is intact, so by using the written and spoken word relearning can slowly take place.

(6) Learning how to learn. Many retraining processes are unsuccessful because the person fails to assimilate specific information. Possibly the goal has been set at too high a level, or is aimed at a particular subject – job, education or even household and daily chores. It is necessary to find a simple task and start at a very simple level. Once the person succeeds and begins to achieve results in the stepwise manner outlined above, the patient begins to appreciate that learning is occurring and the capability is present.

(7) It is essential to identify the patient's deficits clearly. It may require many tests and observations to elicit an individual's specific problems, but it is necessary to do so in order to tailor the retraining effectively.

Behavioural reactions are equally important as they play a part in response. Every rehabilitation programme depends for its success on full consideraton of the individual's needs, strengths and personality.

(8) Feedback. One major complaint in life is the lack of feedback on work or performance. It is always helpful to know if tasks have been performed well, if ideas are useful or if there are changes to be made or errors to be corrected. Without such imformation it is hard to move forward. A little praise works wonders, a careful criticism promotes improvement. So it is crucial that those undergoing retraining should be encouraged as much as possible. It is important to correct errors gently in order to maintain good relationships and not to lower motivation, but praise will help a person to progress. Furthermore, it will help patients to begin again to monitor their performance. This can be a problem particularly with frontal damage, but consistent feedback and comment can have a practice effect and may help the person to improve self monitoring. Expectations can be unrealistic, especially in the early stages, but the mixture of praise and correction can reinforce appropriate responses.

Head injury is an obvious cause of brain damage, but any degenerative condition affects brain function. Each individual's difficulties need to be identified and an appropriate neuropsychological retraining programme should be initiated. To simply conclude that Mr or Mrs Jones has senile dementia is to ensure that deterioration is inevitable. The question **must** be 'What is the cause?'. Once this is estabished the deficits might be easier to discern and a full assessment will clarify the picture. Interventions such as reality orientation and so forth are all very helpful, but they do not provide assistance for neuropsychological deficits unless staff have investigated the probabilities and built in a specific retraining programme for them.

MANAGEMENT

The emotional aspects of degenerative conditions are not to be overlooked and even in the early stages the main considerations should be:

(1) counselling both client and relative;
(2) common sense approaches;
(3) understanding from staff;
(4) a search for retained abilities;
(5) goal setting and parallel intervention policies.

Counselling

Problems lead to anxiety and fear. When patients have insight into their difficulties fear of the future is very real. Relatives experience great anxiety, as they have no idea what the future might hold for them or the changing person that they have known for so long. Explanations are anxiously sought and, in many cases, the need to help is eagerly sought as well. Too often they are informed that little can be done, when what is required is a positive response.

Before any investigation is undertaken the patient should be gently informed that everyone is trying to help and that they are examining every angle in order to do this, furthermore they also understand how upsetting such investigations can be. Once a person is at ease with staff it becomes possible to minimize the effects of anxiety. If a similar explanation is provided for the relatives, it will prove easier to establish the degree of involvement they will offer. They usually want advice and guidelines, so at this stage simple interim procedures can be recommended. The person should be encouraged to do as much as he or she can independently; confidence can be rebuilt by encouragement, by pointing out the successes and the retained skills and abilities that have been in use without the person being conscious of them.

Specific disorders should be given immediate attention, which could include medication, special exercises or advice to continue particular pursuits and interests. Instead of shying away from friends, contact should be maintained. The family, instead of taking over completely, could act in a supportive role, reinforcing independence as much as possible. Staff are advised to take care in the use of pejorative terms which could lead to inaccurate beliefs and poor expectations. If all concerned know that patience and encouragement will result in improved performances, even in small ways, then the person will make better attempts to maintain self care.

The early stages of any condition are important in setting realistic expectation levels.

Common sense approaches

Simple explanations are often overlooked or seen as too simple, yet they can prove the most accurate. For instance if someone gets lost in a large, unfamiliar building the reason could be the lack of direction signs and a normal reaction rather than a loss of the sense of direction. The inability of many hospital patients to tell the day or date is usually interpreted as disorientation, but if there are no calendars, clocks, newspapers or a relevant reason to remember the day and every day seems much the same as another, this is a normal reaction. If someone else takes responsibility for daily chores it soon becomes easier to leave them to it. If a person is left alone for hours on end, if there is no explanation for interference in personal privacy, and there is no personal contact or communication it is hardly surprising if screaming, depression, withdrawal and institutionalization occur.

Commonsense indicates that if strange behaviour occurs that has not been observed previously, careful enquiry should be made. In everyday situations people discourage or reinforce the behaviour of others, even though few are aware of this fact. The comedian who persists in telling a joke at which no one laughs will not proceed very far in the profession. A person makes friends by using warmth and smiles and keeps undesirable acquaintances at a distance by avoiding eye contact and using a flat verbal tone. Such commonplace strategies, once they are entitled **behavior modification**, suddenly become complicated and surrounded in mysticism! These normal responses, once under conscious control, become difficult for relatives to use with a patient. The simple solution of not giving too much attention to a child's minor injury, but using distraction in order to help the child quickly forget about the little pain, is overlooked when the situation involves an elderly adult demanding attention for a variety of unimportant issues.

Many of the problems occurring at home, in residential or hospital settings fall into this category, and yet the obvious response is rarely used. Most of the difficulties unrelated to brain dysfunction can be modified by ignoring the aberrant behaviours and reinforcing the acceptable, natural ones. Even in the rehabilitation or management of patients with specific impairments modification and reinforcement have a major role to play. Praising and encouraging self care attempts and demonstrations of ability will have an effect on motivation and increase the person's will to improve.

Another consideration is the amount of inducement available in the environment. If the atmosphere is sterile, limiting and far removed from normal living, then, obviously, motivation will not blossom. Strict rules, limitations and lack of choice will lead to a person being forced into a pattern of behaviour that causes staff minimum demand, but completely submerges the individual. The environment **must** be active, helpful, stimulating and one which allows normal lifestyles to continue. Each individual should be able to exercise control over the environment.

The search for retained abilities

Global damage only occurs with death; global impairment is unlikely except just prior to death. The amount of retained ability may, in some cases, be small and well hidden, but it is there and it is necessary to find it in order to be of any help to the person. The use of retained abilities is relevant to setting realistic goals and programmes of care. If cognitive, daily living skills and social factors are not clearly identified then goals and rehabilitation plans are doomed to failure.

Goal setting

Realistic goals can be set once assessments are complete and priorities have been established (Barraclough and Fleming, 1985). Aims should be positive, achievable and simple. It is easier to move the goal to a higher level than to attempt to recover the loss occasioned by setting unrealistic aims. As discussed in Chapter 2 targets must be clearly stated, taking all aspects into consideration and not seeking the impossible. They should be in stages, recorded and the person's wishes and priorities included. Goals should extend the person's behaviours rather than limiting them, and he or she should be involved in setting up the programme. Realistic aspirations take into account the severity of the impairments and possibly lack of insight on the part of the patient.

The parallel approach

This simply means team work. Each discipline has something to offer, it is important that ideas should be co-ordinated and specific responsibilities clearly understood. Monitoring of progress is also a group matter. Consistency of approach can minimize conflicting attitudes and interventions.

REHABILITATION AND RETRAINING SUGGESTIONS

Hyperventilation

When first establishing rapport with a patient prior to assessing functions, it may become apparent that the person is hyperventilating. This type of anxious reaction may be the cause of his or her presenting physical problems – palpitations, queasy stomach, dizziness and many other symptoms for which no medical condition has been found. Although this kind of behaviour may not appear relevant to neuropsychological aspects of care, it can have a major bearing on the success or failure of rehabilitative procedures. Furthermore it is not unusual for a patient to be referred to a neurological unit because of particular symptoms: panic attacks, migraine, epilepsy, vertigo, tremor, etc. In order to modify the behaviour, either by eliminating the symptoms or minimizing the anxiety so that rehabilitation programmes can operate, there are some simple exercises that the patient can be taught. An outline of these will be found in Appendix 2 and a more detailed account of hyperventilation is given by Holden (1988).

Briefly, hyperventilation is the result of incorrect breathing, or overbreathing. Breathing is a means of getting oxygen into the blood stream and is the principal way of regulating the acid/base balance of the blood. Overbreathing results in a low level of carbon dioxide, thus provoking respiratory alkalosis. This has, in the past, proved hard to estimate, but now there are improved methods of investigation, e.g. infrared analysers. The various effects of physiological processes are responsible for the production of particular symptoms which will vary from individual to individual. Hyperventilation can frustrate physicians who cannot find a cause for symptoms and frequently patients can be deeply insulted to be told that the problems are imaginary.

Relaxation exercises (refer to Appendix 2) are a part of the technique employed to reduce overbreathing but, instead of the body relaxing technique usually employed, one based on correct, easy breathing is required. Older people find this method easier to follow than other techniques and if rehabilitative programmes are to be introduced these exercises should be well established beforehand and continued throughout.

Case 1

Mrs A was a lady of 76 years. She had suffered a stroke the previous year which had resulted in both expressive and receptive dysphasia. To complicate matters she also had dyspraxia and agnosia. She could not respond to instructions regarding movement tasks, nor did she recognize colours or objects when these were only presented visually. There was a suspicion of left ventricular failure, but the geriatrician felt hyperventilation was a better diagnosis.

A neuropsychological investigation helped to clarify the picture, but provided evidence of yet more deficits which could have a profound effect on treatment programmes. Mrs A did not have real dyspraxia or agnosia, a frontal dysfunction was the cause of these apparent problems. Although aphasia played a major part in her poor comprehension, she perseverated thought and action to a severe degree and logic and sequencing were extremely impaired. When closely observed the reason for her errors and failures was that she was still answering or responding to a question or a task that had been set several minutes before she responded. The question had been mentally taped, but had to take its place on playback before it was its turn for a response! Staff had to remember what had occurred as long as 30 minutes previously before they could understand her remarks, which were already hard to follow because of dysphasia.

Under these circumstances any long explanation was impossible as she was incapable of an appropriate response. Hyperventilation was obvious, as whenever she perceived even minor pressures she began to breathe so fast that she made a series of gasping sounds – roughly 30 breaths a minute.

A simple staged intervention was initiated. Only that part concerning hyperventilation will be outlined here. The use of 'one thousand, two thousand' to slow breathing was obviously too difficult and Mr A, who was in his late 70s, proved too impatient to be of much help, so distraction was used. Observations of the situations which provoked Mrs A's hyperventilation were made and the type of event which made her angry or anxious was recorded. Every time she began to show these reactions a distracting action or remark was used, e.g. 'Oh look, aren't those flowers lovely, don't they smell nice?' or 'You must have had your hair done, it looks lovely, look in the mirror'. To assist understanding, objects and gestures were used too. Mr A found this easy to do and all staff consistently followed this policy. Hyperventilation disappeared remarkably quickly and after 3 months was at least one less problem.

Case 2

Mr T was an apparently fit, healthy and active 82 year old. As a result of his wife's dramatic and colourful accounts of his strange behaviour a full medical examination was carried out. Nothing was found. Mrs T had a history of osteoarthritis and was undoubtedly prone to gross exaggeration. A psychological investigation unearthed a marital problem of many years duration. Mr T had restless, rather anxious behaviour and occasionally dizzy spells when out, but Mrs T appeared more emotionally disturbed. The situation was akin to a folie a deux. Interviews were extremely difficult as each partner insisted on expressing strong views about the other and, if not in the room, was unquestionably listening at the door! The subject of illness dominated all Mrs T's contributions to the discussions.

Their home was attractive and spotless, finacially they had sufficient to allow them to take frequent outings and holidays. However a vicious circle of fault finding had been set up in the early days of marriage and any strategy would necessitate an attempt to divert their attention away from fault to actual enjoyment. Furthermore the constant gasping and sighing from both parties during the interviews required closer attention.

Both were breathing at a rate of at least 24 breaths a minute, both claimed to have noticed the other partner's heavy breathing! The pretty living room had a large wall clock with a second hand. They were taught to use the 'second hand' strategy, to sit down together, at least once a day, and for about 5 minutes to practise easy breathing. They were also to do this before going out, doing something strenuous or before becoming involved in something potentially anxiety provoking.

The couple found this easy to do. They quite enjoyed the idea of having something they could tell the other to do. Their progress was monitored over a 2 month period and they developed a routine which was apparently effective. Mrs T had resented the negative response to her complaints about her husband, but she stopped complaining and actually admitted that her husband had improved. She even felt that her own pains had improved. It was highly unlikely that all would be sweet peace, but they did spend the following summer going out and about and actually enjoyed themselves. After 6 months no further cries for help were heard.

DEGENERATIVE CONDITIONS

Alzheimer's disease and related disorders

Ideally interventions should commence as soon as possible, unfortunately help is often sought only when the problems become well established.

Confidence rebuilding is really the first step. By encouraging the person to do things for him or herself, starting with very simple things, it will be possible to demonstrate success. This will encourage the person to express further independence instead of relinquishing control. Well learned reactions, responses to familiar things, situations and places will aid confidence. It is new material, problems and experiences which provoke anxiety and error.

The environment is an important influence on behaviour. Familiar surroundings and faces are the easiest to recognize and put the person at ease as they are more meaningful and supportive. Well established routines, likes, dislikes and interests play a major part in ensuring that the environment remains a secure and safe place. Too much change can prove catastrophic. Holidays can be very helpful as there is stimulation, but the person does need familiar faces around to help when problems arise. However, the move from one home to another, major changes in staff or even too much change in the house, such as moving furniture round or decorating without consultation or choice, can prove confusing.

Families and carers generally should avoid overprotectiveness or treating an adult like a child. To remove a person's right to self care by washing, dressing and feeding him or her can only lead to greater dependency and an increase in stress for all concerned. There may come a time when this might prove necessary, but it is unwise and improper to ensure that it does. The longer a person retains self responsibility, the longer independence and self esteem will be preserved.

Day-to-day skills, washing up, bed making, dusting, etc., are well learned skills, but they are boring! Each individual has special interests and abilities and these should be used to combat intellectual decline and the pleasant aspect of these abilities requires emphasis. If Mr Smith goes regularily for a drink and to meet his friends in the local pub, then he should be encouraged to continue to do so. To be able to chat with those who have things in common with him can only strengthen his confidence.

When a disease process has reached an advanced stage environmental considerations are especially pertinent (Holden, 1984, 1991). An unhelpful or undemanding environment can accelerate impairments and decline. Simple rules for establishing a useful environment are:

- provide private, recognizable space;
- provide active, interesting and easily identifiable public space;
- make important areas clearly identifiable;
- encourage self care and daily living skills;
- ensure that the decor is bright, cheerful and homely;
- bed areas should be personalized, private and suit the individual;
- the individual should have reasonable control over the environment;
- ensure that social contacts are possible and encourage group identity;
- there should be something interesting to do; evenings are not just an extension of daytime or a time to doze.
- relevant information should be readily available – calendars, clocks, events, news, etc.

The use of reality orientation (Holden and Woods, 1988, 1995; Hanley, 1988), reminiscence (Norris, 1986; Coleman, 1986), group living (Rothwell *et al.*, 1983; Booth and Phillips, 1987) and the various exercise, music, drama and movement therapies, plus other approaches, are relevant aids to memory, orientation and the maintenance of abilities, skills and sociability. They also make some impact on the degree of dementia (Charatan, 1984).

It is also vital to establish the real diagnosis of a person with dementia. The outlines of symptoms and signs provided in the chapters on the 'new' dementias will be of assistance when the problems are unclear. To treat someone with a frontal dementia or a Lewy body disease in the same way as someone who has an Alzheimer type condition will not provide that person with the most useful support or help.

For instance, if Mrs Green has a frontal dementia she will have many preserved functions that differ from those of a person with AD. She will be able to converse and understand current events, care for herself with prompting and do many of the tasks and interests that she had before the changes occurred. Concentration needs to be placed on explanations to her and her family and then on finding ways to manage the difficulties imposed by frontal damage.

Mr Glover, on the other hand, has a Lewy body disease, so it is only during the periods of confusion that he poses problems. Understanding this and the probable hallucinatory experiences will assist both him and the family to concentrate on the lucid periods and maintain his abilities for as long as possible.

Each of these differing conditions requires a different approach and any rehabilitation team does need to know as much as possible about the neuropsychological deficits and possible ways to treat or manage them.

MID

It is vital to identify preserved abilities and functions when a person has suffered from a vascular accident. The shock and distress of both patient and relatives require calming and minimizing before any rehabilitative programme can be introduced. The next stage is a full and careful neuropsychological investigation. Is language preserved or damaged, is there any sensory deficit? If language impairments are present it will be necessary to improve communication by the use of pictorial material with minimal language in partnership. If spatial and perceptual difficulties are the main impairments then language becomes the main medium for retraining.

It is helpful if staff remain aware of the fact that a stroke does not necessarily mean that an elderly person will not recover or will suffer from severe permanent damage. A person's future is in jeopardy if no one believes that recovery is possible. Patients who have had very serious or series of strokes causing numerous deficits may well have sustained such damage as will interfere with their capacity to cope with independent living but, even then, there will be certain retained functions which can be used to assist the person to maintain some degree of independence and self confidence.

It is not always easy to identify retained or temporarily out of action functions. It may well require a great deal of patient observation and enquiry, plus considerable effort, to elicit co-operation from the patient. The hardest thing for a therapist to accept is a person's refusal to co-operate. If motivation cannot be aroused, if the person clearly chooses to withdraw, to make no effort to improve functioning, or even chooses to die, then there is nothing anyone can do to force events to change. An individual has the right to choose and no one can interfere with that choice. Alternatives can be made obvious and appealing, and the individual should be given the opportunity to consider them, but in the end it is that person who must make the decision. All staff can do in such circumstances is to provide warmth, good care and patience – the person may change his or her mind as a result. Staff need to give each other support and feel free to talk about the situation. Feelings of guilt and inadequacy are not appropriate.

Sub-cortical states

Obviously each disorder poses different problems and requires a slightly different approach. AIDS, for instance, will fall in the realms of a separate specialty, though staff involved should have a working knowledge of elderly care in order to meet the particular needs of that age group. As with all patients, the individual will always be different. However, there are a few general points to be considered:

- It is necessary to appreciate that intellectual ability will be preserved until very late in the course of the disease process.
- Slow, or even lack of, response does not signify an inability to respond nor a lack of motivation.
- If the reactions of others are impatience, irritability or dismissal the patient will become withdrawn, depressed or even despairing.
- If distractions or ways to split concentration on a task are employed the patient will be able to respond more easily.

> Mr Brown had Parkinson's disease and often found it hard to get started, the staff arranged to have footsteps printed on the ground for a few paces in front of his chair. He was encouraged to sing to himself 'Put your right foot in and shake it all about, put your left foot in . . .'. It got him started and once up and moving he had no further problem walking about.

- Encourage response, give the person time and do not accept comments such as 'I don't know' if there is a possibility that this is due to the experience gained from encountering other people's impatience.

With some conditions, such as progressive supranuclear palsy, occupational therapists and physiotherapists can be of great assistance in providing aid for dysphagia (swallowing difficulties), book stands at higher levels so that the person can continue to read in comfort and other methods to provide head supports or safety measures to prevent falling.

Family and friends

There are many associations which provide information and support concerning differing conditions. Families should be given information on how to contact relevant local and national societies. However, the unit directly involved with an individual should also be capable of providing written guidelines for that individual's special needs. It is too easy for clients and relatives to forget all the advice that has been discussed in an interview. Standard handouts require careful scrutiny before being passed on as it may not prove appropriate for a particular patient and efforts should be made to tailor it accordingly. For instance the suggested guidelines in the Appendices will not be suitable for every individual and will need amending. The persòn may be functioning at a higher or lower level, so it is necessary to pick out the ideas that are relevant, cross out the others or even produce a totally new set of guidelines. Packages can be taken as law!

To suggest to a poorly paid family that they are required to purchase expensive elctronic games would be unrealistic and unfair. However, there are many games on the market which can make relearning a pleasure and something all the family can enjoy. Some of them are electronic and some of them are reasonably priced items that might be bought for family amusement, but they can also be geared to using specific skills such as memory, hand–eye co-ordination, spatial perception and the use of language. If a person has only minimal deficits and is of a high intellectual level something more stimulating than household chores is required to increase motivation. To aid language skills games such as Scrabble, Lexicon Cards, Trivial Pursuit, quizzes generally, crosswords, etc., can all prove invaluable.

Spatial difficulties can benefit from three-dimensional games such as Spacelines, Connect 4, mosaics, jigsaws and so forth. There is a wide range of memory games, including electronic ones such as Wizard, Adam and Simon. On a simpler level, shopping lists, prices, calcuation of bills and the use of diaries can be recomended. With the help of relatives a person could make notes on an interesting item of news on the radio and follow it up during the day, trying to remember it before the next news, reinforcing it with the next news and either adding to it or trying again at the next bulletin. Newspapers and television could add another opportunity on the same item and the family could ask the person to recall the information without recourse to notes, or with them if necessary.

More severely impaired people living at home would need simple reminders. A basic reality orientation (RO) approach could be implemented, with calendars, notice boards and repetition. Repetition must not be parrot-like, but the same information conveyed in different ways to enable it to be absorbed, for example: 'It's time to get up', '8.30 Dad, how are you getting on?' 'Breakfast is ready, are you coming?'. Each remark is different, but all are telling Dad to get up. Information can be imparted again and again without actually repeating the same words. This allows the person time to grasp the necessary concept and helps relatives to avoid the frustration caused by saying the same thing over and over again.

It will also prove helpful if relatives try to reinforce success: 'You did that well' or 'Quite right Mum' is more encouraging than 'You can do that better' or 'You used to be able to do that'. The more a confused person believes success is still possible, the more likely it is that he or she will attempt simple self care tasks.

SPECIFIC DEFICITS

> Remediating cognitive deficit remains the greatest challenge to those concerned with rehabilitation.
>
> *Diller, 1976*

Rehabilitation sessions should be short, frequent, interesting to the client and require plenty of praise, feedback and encouragement. They can last from 30 to 60 minutes, can take place at home, in a home, on a ward or in a day unit, but they must occur or progress will be limited to the whims of nature and the person's level of motivation.

Orientation and attention

Many confused people ramble, talk nonsense and do not appear to give sensible replies to questions. A simple remedy is to use good eye contact, slow speech and gentle touch on an arm or a hand. If a question is put clearly in this way an appropriate reply will almost cetainly be the result. The length of time that attention lasts will vary and it will probably be necessary to use the strategy again, but once attention is lost a break is indicated. However, the use of this method on a regular basis will provide practice and the span will slowly lengthen.

Time sense will be assisted by a large, clear clock placed where it can be seen. It will require reminders to look at it until the person learns to look without a prompt. Calendars and notice boards can be used to highlight specific events such as holidays, special events, meal times and favourite TV programmes. Few people remember actual days with ease unless there is some kind of tag: Monday is going to work day, Friday is pay day, Saturday and Sunday are weekends, etc. In care situations most days are like one another, so it is advisable to find a reason for people to remember.

> One unit organized the week on the basis of which four patients would have the use of a special room for the day. This room allowed the residents to look after themselves, have their meals separately, wash up, watch their own TV or interest themselves as they chose. Everyone always knew what day it was because they were protective of their opportunity to take over 'the room.'

Orientation with regard to place can be improved by the use of direction signs, notices, pictures, photographs, maps and views from a window. However, it is vital to ensure that patients are taught how to use them and given the opportunity to learn to look by prompting from staff or relatives. Aids are of little use if the patients are unaware of their existence. There are several resource centres which provide pictures of particular places, such as supermarkets, bus stations, main street shops, and which also provide photographs which can be sorted to match the correct place.

Orientation concerning the person strictly implies self recognition. The consistent use of the patient's name, photographs and mirrors can prove helpful.

Aphasias

Dysphasias are the provence of speech therapy and more detailed accounts of assessments and treatment can be obtained from books by Ulatowska (1985) and Gravell (1988). Here a more general approach will be outlined. A person suffering from dysphasia is in the unenviable position of being unable to express feelings, ideas or needs satisfactorily. Each individual will have a specific difficulty as well as retained ability; it is necessary to attempt to identify both aspects in order to find ways to help.

When language is impaired there are multiple effects:

- social contacts and outlets are limited;
- understanding of and by a person are limited;
- other methods of communication are required;
- relatives and staff can overlook the individual personality and conclude the person requires total care;
- basic intelligence is assumed to be lost;
- the person is probably depressed, but certainly frequently frustrated.

So it is essential to:

- help others to appreciate the hidden intelligence **and** the individual;
- speak slowly, clearly and simply to aid understanding;
- explain any intervention;
- give the person time to comprehend or respond;
- use other means of communication, e.g. gesture, pictures, writing, letters or matching; speech may improve, perhaps only one word at a time;
- use retained and spatial or perceptual abilities; when a person looks at a picture or picks up an object, name it, try to encourage the person to repeat the name, or at least to recognize the word. Use single words, verbally or written, in relation to all objects, events, pictures in order to

help relearning of language skills. Speech may not improve, there may be a little improvement, or the person may simply begin to relate objects to words to some extent.

Frequently staff and relatives are unaware of the fact that messages are understood even though words may not be. Tone, rhythm, emphasis, gesture, melody and music are not governed by the language area of the brain, they belong to another system in the other hemisphere. So the tone that is used and the way things are said can be meaningful to a dysphasic individual. Patronizing tones, pejorative remarks and dismissive gestures are all probably understood and can only make a person become more depressed, despairing or angry. Whereas if gesture and tone are used to convey messages and some information to the person this could prove an effective way to help.

It is not advisable to include a person with receptive dysphasia in group activities. A one-to-one situation is usually more effective. To see others responding, understanding and, particularly, laughing at a joke can precipitate depression and feelings of despair. If a patient has an expressive dysphasia it is possible to include him or her in a group, as long as great care is taken to find means to assist involvement. Perhaps the person can write, draw or use pictorial material. If not, gesture might be appropriate. He or she will understand most of the conversation, but the difficulty will be in joining in, therefore some method suitable for that person must be found.

Although it is preferable to call on the advice and aid of a speech therapist, it is not always possible to do this. For those interested in some of the retraining programmes that they have provided, Winslow Press offer a number of useful books, exercise plans and workbooks, e.g. *Working with Dysphasics* (Faucus *et al.*, 1984) and *Aphasia Therapy in Practice* (Faucus *et al.*, 1992).

Apraxias

Although this problem is frequently present, often overlooked and usually misinterpreted it is difficult to find relevant information on management or treatment techniques. More research and practical ideas regarding dyspraxia for speech have been produced, Melodic Intonation Therapy (Sparks and Holland, 1976) being a relevant example. This system essentially uses a form of distraction, or split attention, in order to assist a patient with dyspraxia for speech to be able to produce words again. Simply, the person is taught to sing what has to be said. The need to think of a tune as well as words appears to aid many patients with this problem. In a similar way distraction can be utilized with movement disorders.

It is vital to avoid giving an apraxic patient direct instructions about performing a task or action. To tell a person 'Pick up your knife and fork', or 'Put your hand through here . . . put your foot in there' will almost certainly lead to failure. With very deteriorated patients it is advisable to avoid direct instructions and allow automatic responses to take place. If giving a person a cup of tea instead of saying 'There's your tea Mrs S, drink it up', just place the cup within sight and make a general comment, automatically Mrs S will pick up the cup. However, when a patient has retained most abilities and can respond to learning strategies for self help, the use of rhythm and melody are valuable. If the person is taught to sing or hum a tune to him or herself, or beat time simultaneously with the action required, success is more likely to occur. Another person can do the singing, humming or time beating, but in due course the person should learn to do this alone. To the chant of 'up and down, up and down' the patient may giggle, but teeth get cleaned! Having more than one action or idea to consider removes the degree of voluntary focus from the action.

> Mrs Flynn had a minor stroke but unfortunately, although recovering well, she had great difficulty in carrying out tasks on request. When asked to brush her teeth, for example, she found it impossible. She was taught to hum a lively tune in her head – the nurse sang it for her first – and try to brush her teeth simultaneously. This proved successful. She also found it useful to tap her foot at the same time as performing a requested task.

Luria (1963) provided a number of strategies, but there has been little or no attempt to replicate them. The ideas offered here have proved of use in clinical practice, but they might not be of value in every case. As Luria stressed, it is important to observe the individual and note when difficulties arise, what happens, what response is made, does the patient plan, break the task into stages or even understand what is expected? If a person is very disabled or demented it is difficult to assess the process of response and even whether an apraxia is present, as there may be post-trauma weakness or hemiplegia.

Peripheral weakness or lack of full control is the province of physiotherapists, but apart from graded exercises there are some game-like tasks which can assist as well. A minature piano can be used to improve finger strength; stacking plastic or paper cups, sorting buttons into sets or cutting out pictures or materials for a collage are useful ways to exercise the fingers and hands. Those with slight dyspraxia might also benefit from these exercises, though some guiding of the hands or miming will be required before a person can get started.

The use of pictorial material with minimal verbal instructions is another approach. A series of pictures showing how to do something – shaving, making a telephone call, making a sandwich – demonstrates what is required without actual verbal instructions. This can serve to split concentration between performing the action and following the pictorial sequence and possibly some verbal instruction. If words are actually written on the pictures, spoken instructions may not be necessary and the presence or absence of a language disability is not a problem.

The agitation or apparent resistance of a person when staff or relatives are trying to feed or dress him/her may not be a form of aggression but, in fact, frustration, and the resistant actions may be an attempt to perform the task, but unfortunately the movements are not appropriate. It is important to observe exactly what is occurring. Are staff or relatives telling the person what to do? Is the person using movements that are opposite to those required? Is the person making any correct response to directions or are they verbalizing anger, annoyance or distress? The rigid clenching of fists can be the result of a conscious attempt to perform a task. For instance, after shaking hands with a patient a doctor may say 'I'm going now Mrs S. I hope all goes well, goodbye', but instead of releasing the hand Mrs S clutches even harder. A change of conversation or a diversional tactic will soon release the clasp: 'That is a pretty ring you have on your finger' will be enough for her to let go to make some comment such as 'My husband gave me that on my birthday'.

Relatives and staff could find it more productive to talk about the look and taste of food, or even about the state of the weather, than to give an apraxic person direct instructions on how to eat the food. Sometimes miming an action can spark off a correct response; demonstrating with actual objects can also help. A touch of humour can prove invaluable as a distraction.

Constructinal apraxia may be helped in a similar manner: pictorial material in a how to do it series, giving the person time to think, helping them to plan each step and by using simple family games to obtain practice. Jigsaws for adults, making collages, mosaics, even Lego for building little houses can all be put to use.

Dressing apraxia can be due to many different impairments and individuals may have very different problems. It will be necessary to try a number of strategies before an effective intervention can be found. For example:

- Colour: red tabs on the back of clothes; a yellow tab marked left for the left shoe and red for the right one.
- Order: laying the clothes out in the order in which that individual usually dresses
- Spoken instructions, with a guiding hand: talk through each stage whilst using a prompting gesture. Start the person off, then allow him or her to finish putting on each item.
- Mime: pretend to put something on.

- Demonstrate: actually put on, or start to put on an item, then hand it to the person.

Aims should be low at first, allowing the person to do as much alone as possible, giving lots of time, correcting mistakes as they arise. Work step by step and provide encouragement and praise for each little success. It may take time before progress is made, but it is important to take that time in order to ensure that dressing skills are relearned. It is preferable to find a solution to the problem than to have to spend time continually dressing and undressing a person and by so doing extending dependency.

Spatial disorders

Losing the way, even in familiar places, can cause frustration and anxiety, not only for relatives and staff but also for the patient. In severe cases the starting point for retraining could be drawing rooms and the use of cut outs of furniture and equipment. The person could be asked to put together a kitchen, sitting room or bedroom, placing the pieces of furniture in appropriate places. When this is done he or she could be asked 'Is this like your room at home?'.

Attempts to replicate the rooms at home could be the next stage. He or she can be asked:

'How do you find your way to the bedroom/toilet/kichen, etc.?'
'What are the colours of the walls/carpets in . . .?'
'What materials/textures are used for curtains/furnishings?'
'What style/shape is your furniture in the living room . . .?'

This can provoke associations and help the person to recall forgotten clues. At a later stage drawing maps at increasing levels of difficulty could be tried, for example:

- the street on which the person lives;
- the main shopping street, showing the supermarket, post office, newsagent, etc.;

Real photographs can be used which will make the exercise more realistic and interesting. Larger maps of the entire country can be introduced and major towns and places identified. World maps are also relevant.

Equipment for these relearning programmes can be made from magazines or obtained from many resource agencies including Winslow Press.

Other useful guides include painting coloured lines along walls to direct a person to the toilet. Patterns and colours for doors also assist identification. Orientation, as outlined previously, is improved by direction signs with both words and pictures; a familiar picture or object hung on or by a bedroom door will help a person to recognise his or her own room. New residents will be confused by strange surroundings so it is important to teach them to find their way about. To simply point out the signs and provide a single tour will not be sufficient. Clues need to be pointed out again and again, and then the person should take the staff to different locations so that mistakes can be corrected and the layout properly learned (Hanley, 1981).

Confusion in the home can be aided by the use of little pictures and words placed in relevant positions. Cutlery, clothing, linen and jewellery, for example, can all be found and replaced if the person has clues to where things go. As in ward training constant reminders about the clues will be necessary at first. When clients live alone, home organizers, or visiting nursing staff, can act as guides and reinforcers until a routine is established.

There are many games in which space plays a part that can be purchased in local shops: Spacelines, Connect 4, Trac 4, for instance. Painting, drawing, mosaics and collages will provide practice in handling spatial tasks.

Agnosias

Perceptual errors can prove confusing and anxiety provoking for both client and relative. The solution to most object agnosias is really quite simple, but other deficits might complicate the situation. As in all cases of brain damage, the problems vary from person to person and it is extremely difficult for the observer to appreciate the difficulties even a most intelligent person with agnosia is experiencing. Some patients are unable to structure what they see, some use logic to solve the puzzle, some find it humorous, others are depressed. Often when the person is encouraged to use the preserved senses an object can be recognized. If the problem is with sight, by using touch, hearing or smell it becomes obvious what the object is, but if the object is in the distance, identification becomes almost impossible and only logic can help.

Agnosia for touch will be assisted by sight, but if it is dark sight alone is insufficient. The person will have to learn to associate the object with a particular clue. For instance, a door key could have a rough string attached to it and it could be the only item in a particular pocket or pouch in a handbag.

Auditory agnosia for speech can be assisted if everyone speaks at a slower pace, giving the person time to assimilate what is said. The normal rate of speech is too fast, but once it is slowed down the person's comprehension is improved. Agnosia for non-verbal sounds can be dangerous as the person needs to see the source of the sound in order to identify it. It is unfortunate that barking dogs cannot be persuaded to bark more slowly, and it is equally impossible to influence the rate of noise made by objects so this form of agnosia remains a problem.

Body image disturbances

In the acute form these may be short lived, but some degree of difficulty will persist.

Unilateral neglect is a common form and has received much attention regarding both the cause and possible treatments. It is important not to reinforce neglect of one side of the body, but it is useless to attempt retraining by working with the person from the neglected side. This can only guarantee a total lack of response. On the other hand to begin by working directly in front of the person will help. As with drawing circles, in most cases, if part can be perceived, the whole will be too. This does not always occur, as for example with a plate of food – the person may only eat half and will not be aware of the rest unless the plate is turned around. Possibly some form of logic is involved.

Robertson, Halligan and Marshall (1993) provide a useful chapter on rehabilitation of unilateral neglect which suggests that with many programmes it is possible for the person to relearn a way to manage one type of problem but, unfortunately, the success may not be generated to other situations. In clinical practice it has been found useful to supply the patient with a brightly coloured stick which is placed at the point on a book, journal or document where the person can begin to read. By distracting attention and moving the stick slightly into the neglected field of vision the person can be asked to 'Read from the coloured stick'. This can slowly improve the person's awareness of the neglected side. Robertson *et al.* quote several studies which found this method to be successful. Unfortunately this awareness does not generalize into other needs of awareness of that side.

It has also proved successful to place large coloured paper markers on the edges of tables and other obstacles with which a person may regularly collide. Once this process of avoidance has been learned the markers can be removed and collisions cease. Once again, this will not generalize into areas where training has not taken place.

Joanette *et al.* (1986) found that if the limb contralateral to the lesion was used to point to a target neglect was less severe than when the limb ipsilateral (to the same side) to the lesion was used. Robertson *et al.* (1993) reported three studies with patients who were trained to:

(a) always place the left partially hemiplegic arm (with the aid of the right hand) to the left of any activity and to locate it visually each time;
(b) place a buzzer to the left of any activity, its noise to be terminated by the patient pressing a large switch with the hemiplegic left hand; and
(c) undertake a similar task to (b), without the need to scan for the position of the left arm.

In all cases improvements were generalized to everyday life as well as the experimental situation.

Robertson and North (1992), in a series of experiments, found that by getting a finger of the neglected side to move in the neglected left hemi-space the degree of neglect was improved. In other words mobilizing a part of the hemiplegic side, even a finger, was a major feature of any attempt to lessen neglect.

Prosopagnosia and **simultanagnosia** are both extremely hard to treat. With the former many strategies are required as there can be an element of rejection in some cases. It may be convenient to claim that an annoying husband or wife is a stranger!

Body image disturbances may respond if the person is asked to touch his or her own nose, cheek, hair, etc., while looking in the mirror. The use of photographs, matching and the sound of familiar voices with the 'forgotten' faces can often help. Occasionally it has proved successful to find that a husband and wife have a special secret unknown to anyone else. Surprisingly, using this secret can help the partner, who has failed to recognize the spouse, to realize who she must be. Logic is obviously preserved!

Where it is difficult for a person to distinguish one object from another, ensure that important things are not close together and that objects are laid out in an orderly manner. Use a peaceful area for retraining. Train the person to move his or her head in order to improve scanning. Use games which focus on particular senses, for example ask the person to describe the object he or she feels in a bag without being able to see it, then use sight as well. Retraining of shapes and colours can be aided by feel, drawing and discussion plus sight.

If the person is suffering from Balint's syndrome a combination of agnosias will be present. Understanding the person's difficulties will assist relatives and they can be encouraged to use some of the strategies outlined above. Simply moving objects into view, using brightly coloured circles or squares on objects to draw attention to their existence and employing senses other than sight will meet some of the needs. A guiding hand will allow a person to pick something up effectively, but various methods will have to be attempted before finding those that are relevant to the individual.

Memory

This is considered a major problem and occurs even in the early stages of some disease processes. As a result it has received more attention than many other impairments. Theoretical aspects have received the greatest input and those readers with an interest in the mechanisms, theories and details of retraining programmes should consult work by Wilson (1987), Wilson and Moffat (1992), Miller and Morris (1993) or Stokes (1992).

Various studies have identified that verbal rehearsal of material does assist memory, as long as there is no interference. Patients with a dementia appear to have impairments in encoding (entering memory) and in retrieval of information. However, as in reminisence therapy, 'overlearning', frequent rehearsal or often recounted experiences do ensure that certain memories remain 'evergreen'. Recent studies have also shown that when there is something spectacular or particularly notable, these are stored and retrieved with comparative ease. For instance when patients were asked to recall the names of previous prime ministers, Mrs Thatcher's name was produced more frequently than any other!

Wilson (1987) and Wilson and Moffat (1992) have provided accounts of useful memory therapies and guidelines on setting up and running memory groups which have become popular throughout the country. These are occsionally called memory clinics (Van Der Cammen *et al.* 1987; Twining 1991). Wilson and Moffat distinguish between the groups run for elderly people complaining of memory loss without major cognitive impairment and for those with some form of dementia. The latter are more appropriately helped by reality orientation and reminiscence group work, or with specific retraining to meet a particular need. Planned programmes are provided by Hanley (1988) whose client wished to remember that her husband had died, and Holden and Woods (1988, 1995) describe various retraining plans for patients who complained of a poor memory.

Although it is extremely difficult to obtain great improvements in memory where functions have sustained damage, there are ways to help and there are cases of pseudo-memory loss. Emotional factors and expectations can interfere with concentration and motivation. Depression or apathy leads to disinterest, illness to frailty and expectation to benign forgetfulness. In such instances real memory loss has not occurred. It is important to establish the true nature of a reported memory loss as soon as possible so a suitable approach can be employed.

A very relevant study (Levy and Langer, 1994) found that cultural patterns and influences had a major bearing on an older person's expectations regarding memory. They compared older Americans who could hear with those who were deaf and older people from China. Their hypothesis was that those who were deaf would not be aware of negative social stereotypes and the Chinese came from a culture which venerated age and therefore had not experienced ageism. The older American deaf and the Chinese subjects outperformed the Americans without hearing problems on the memory tasks. There was a positive correlation between attitudes to ageing and memory performance. Levy and Langer concluded that stereotypes result in self fulfilling prophecies as people expect the worst and do not involve themselves in activities which can help to maintain ability.

Memory problems require programmes which are designed for the individual, may include group work utlilizing well learned social skills and which offer pleasant experiences in order to stimulate motivation and response. The form of retraining will depend on the person, past skills and experiences, the problem and retained abilities.

Perceptions are usualy taken for granted and little attention is paid to ordinary experiences such as the colour of the neighbour's door, the number of steps to the stairs or even the route taken by a driver. In residential homes the residents often cannot tell where rooms other than their own are located and should be encouraged to take note of little cues so that they can be independent in finding their way around. Staff should regularly train new arrivals to note the colour of corridors, direction signs, clocks, directions to the toilet and so forth. Those living at home should be reminded of the simple things which will help them remember where everything is situated or stored. Previously it may have been possible to think of something else when going to the grocer's shop, now it is important to take note of street names, the house on a corner, the name of the hotel and everything that can be used as a cue to finding the way.

Diaries and notebooks are important, but they must be used and not left in a drawer. Notice boards in the kitchen, or in a care setting, should have updated information and be in daily use. Prompts by staff and relatives will encourage the person to be aware and think about what is happening: 'What did you have for breakfast today?' 'Who is coming to see you this afternoon?'; 'What are you going to watch on television tonight?' Games of all kinds can make practice more palatable and more fun.

Frontal damage

Some of the problem behaviours associated with frontal lobe damage have already been covered in this and other chapters. Here only the behavioural problems particularily common amongst older people will be considered.

Perseveration

It can be very distressing and irritating to be the observer of persistent and oft repeated actions, questions, statements or phrases. Staff, friends, relatives and other residents can find such situations hard to tolerate and perseveration is a major factor in causing stress reactions. Many strategies have been attempted to minimize the repetition, but few have proved successful. Although there is difficulty in finding helpful strategies there are some methods which can be considered, and sometimes assumptions about the cause of perseveration may be incorrect.

Occasionally this persistence has nothing to do with frontal damage and may well be due to actual loneliness. It is important that people should not be isolated for too long without anything to do, or any company. For instance the repeated phrases can occur when the person has been left alone for long periods of time and eventually the annoying words will prompt a response from someone. Usually it is far from warm or friendly, but at least it is a response!

In either case – actual loneliness or actual frontal damage – staff could set up key workers, to cover all hours of the day if necessary, with a specific programme which is understood by all staff members and relatives. The person should be given attention when he or she is **not** repeating words or phrases and ignored when doing so, but the length of time he or she is left alone should be monitored and kept to a reasonable length. Other residents should be informed of this too. Unfortunately, it is often the other residents who can cause failure with this approach as it can be impossible for them to refrain from abusive responses to the constant parrot talk!

Several studies have attempted to record the perseverative talk and then play it back to the speaker. The voice is not recognized and the usual reaction is 'For God's sake, shut up' from the perseverator him or herself!

Luria used interruptions with movements in order to prevent motor perseveration. This can be equally successful with the verbal form. As the irritating word, phrase or sentence begins, some form of distraction can be introduced. According to the situation and the individual involved a comment, noise or touch can be a distraction. 'Oh, Mrs Lane, look at these lovely flowers', or 'Mr Cross, look the football results are on this page in the newspaper' are possible comments. The ensuing normal conversation will provide an opportunity to give the person some attention and encouragement so that more acceptable behaviours can be reinforced. A gentle hand on the person's arm or hand, with a warm tone in the voice, can also work wonders.

Thought can become one track too. The most effective way to manage the 'stuck needle syndrome' is to find ways to lift the needle and let thought move on. Years ago when the needle stuck with the old gramophone it would play on when someone jumped on the floor beside the machine. In the case of a person stuck with a thought, staff or relatives can use a loud hand clap, drop something noisily, ring a bell or do something which will startle the person sufficiently to interrupt the thought process and allow new material to be understood and normal conversation to proceed.

When gesture or movement is being repeated it is necessary to interrupt completion or continuation of the movement by a restraining hand. This should be done as soon as the gesture commences, accompanied by warmth and interest in the person, including staying to talk for a while.

It is advisable to check the degree of stimulation available in the environment. If nothing is happening stereotyped behaviour is not uncommon. Even in zoos caged animals can express neurotic behaviour if they are in a poor and unsuitable environment. Any sterile atmosphere can lead to psychological distress, so before any specific intervention is employed with an individual it is imperative to ascertain if it is in response to the poverty of the environment rather than to actual brain damage.

Poor seqeuncing ability

An impairment in organization, in putting things into a logical order, is often seen with head injured clients; it also occurs with frontal lobe dementia and other conditions affecting older people. Staged practice in putting things into order can help a little. Breaking a task down into its component parts and drawing the person's attention to each separate part is one method. A set of pictures or cartoons with either directions on how to perform a task or which tell a story can be mixed up and the person asked to place them correctly and meaningfully. Usually it is wise to start with only two pictures and simple concepts. Occupational therapy material provides sets of pictures on the seasons, how to make a sandwich, to shave, make a phone call, etc., and these can be ideal. Newspapers and journals have cartoons which can be cut out and sorted appropriately by the patient. As improvement occurs the standard can be raised and more complicated concepts employed, e.g. the stages in the growth of a plant or cake making.

It is necessary to demonstrate to the person that he or she really can use order, so investigations should seek to identify such preserved ability. Can the person dress him or herself, wash independently or perform other daily living skills without aid? When these are identified they should be brought to the attention of the patient and the self ordering success stressed as encouragement and reinforcement.

Logical thinking is also affected. The use of sequence retraining will be one way to improve this a little. Game-like sessions on planning daily or weekly menus, planning the day's chores and actual games which demand planning and logical processes, e.g. Cluedo, are appropriate.

RECORDING, EVALUATION AND SERVICES

As there is so much variation from individual to individual in the type and degree of dysfunction, it is important to record the progress of all interventions, also the reason for them. What might be suitable for one person may prove useless with another. If, after a reasonable trial period, an approach does not show any improvement in the behaviour or problem, then it is time to discuss other approaches. However, as some of the behaviours may be well established, or because there might be a lack of consistency or interference in the present system, careful scrutiny of the manner in which the programme has been conducted should be made before any changes are introduced.

As there is still a paucity of techniques to improve neuropsychological deficits in elderly people, careful recording could lead to evaluation studies and a greater number of relevant approaches available to therapists. In a 'new' field, new ideas are required. Sadly, though many therapists have successful methods of their own, there appears to be a reluctance to publish in popular journals so that the staff actually working with patients can be informed and try out some of these procedures themselves. Single case studies can be of great assistance and evaluation may simply consist of showing that a particular approach worked with an individual. Staff need the encouragement to use their imagination in conjunction with knowledge.

Day hospitals for elderly people require staff who are trained in rehabilitation techniques. Respite care is the role of units other than day hospitals. Day centres, residential homes and certain wards are responsible for this important aspect of care, but not day hospitals. The latter are responsible for physical care problems as well as finding the means to maintain a person at a good level of functioning, identifying ways to manage and treat specific deficits and impairments, counselling patients and relatives and providing programmes which will improve, control or compensate for specific neuropsychological deficits. The day hospital that does not provide this is not cost effective and the services offered could be supplied by another agency. Furthermore in order to be able to carry out these responsibilities the staff require training, updating and a flow of new ideas on methods to use for particular impairments. Apart from the lack of appreciation for rehabilitation staff or general understanding of their role, they do not receive enough training, resources or opportunities to update on research findings or useful new methods. In order to provide the necessary service and minimize the number of dependent elderly people, hospital management should make this a major concern.

REFERENCES

Barraclough, C. and Fleming, I. (1985) *Goal Setting With Elderly People*, Manchester University Press, Manchester.

Booth, T. and Phillips, D. (1987) Group living in homes for the elderly: a comparative study of outcome of care. *British Journal of Social Work*, **17**, 1–20.

Charatan, E.B. (1984) Mental stimulation and deprivation of risk factors in senility, in *Risk Factors in Senility*, (ed. H. Rothschild), Oxford University Press, New York.

Coleman, P. (1986) *Ageing and Reminiscence Processes: Social and Clinical Implications*, Wiley, Chichester and New York.

Craine, J.F. (1987) Principles of cognitive rehabilitation, in *Cognitive Rehabilitation: Conceptualization and Intervention*, (ed. L.E. Trexler), Plenum Press, New York.

Faucus, M., Kerr, J., Whitehead, S. and Williams, R.A. (1992) *Aphasia Therapy in Practice*, Series of 3: Expression; Comprehension; Reading, Winslow Press, Oxford.

Faucus, M., Robinson, M., Williams, J. and Williams, R. (1984) *Working with Dysphasics*, Winslow Press, Oxford.

Gravell, R. (1988) *Communication Problems in Elderly People*, Chapman & Hall, London.

Hanley, I.G. (1981) The use of signposts and active training to modify ward disorientation in elderly patients. *Journal of Behaviour Therapy And Experimental Psychiatry*, **12**, 241–7.

Hanley, I.G. (1988) *Individualized Reality Orientation*, via Winslow Press, Oxford.

Holden, U.P. (1984) *Thinking it Through*, Winslow Press, Oxford.

Holden, U.P. (ed.) (1988) *Neuropsychology and Ageing*, Croom Helm, London.

Holden, U.P. (1991) *Day into Night*, Winslow Press, Oxford.

Holden, U.P. and Woods, R.T. (1988) *Reality Orientation; Psychological Approaches to the 'Confused' Elderly*, 2nd ed, Churchill Livingstone, Edinburgh.

Holden, U.P. and Woods, R.T. (1995) *Positive Approaches to Dementia Care*, Churchill Livingstone, Edinburgh.

Joanette, Y., Brouchon, M. Gauthier, I. and Samson, M. (1986) Pointing with left versus right hand in left visual field neglect. *Neuropsychologica*, **24**, 391–6.

Kitwood, T. (1993) Towards a theory of dementia care: the interpersonal process. *Ageing and Society*, **13**, 51–67.

Levy, B. and Langer, E. (1994) Ageing free from negative stereotypes: successful memory in China and among the American deaf. *Journal of Personality and Social Psychology*, **66**, 989–97.

Luria, A.R. (1963) *Restoration of Function after Brain Injury*, Pergamon Press, Oxford.

Luria, A.R., Naydin, V.L., Tsvetkova, L.S. and Vinarskaya, E.N. (1969) Restoration of higher cortical function following local brain damage, in *Handbook of Clinical Neurology*, Vol. 3, (eds R.S. Vinken and G.W. Bryn), North Holland, Amsterdam.

Miller, E. (1984) *Recovery and Management of Neuropsychological Impairments*, Churchill Livingstone, Edinburgh.

Miller, E. and Morris, R. (1993) *The Psychology of Dementia*, Wiley, Chichester.

Muir Giles, G. and Clark-Wilson, J. (1993) *Brain Injury Rehabilitation: A Neurofunctional Approach*, Chapman & Hall, London.

Norris, A. (1986) *Reminiscence with Elderly People*, Winslow Press, Oxford.

Robertson, I.H., Halligan, P.W. and Marshall, J.C. (1993) Prospects for the rehabilitation of unilateral neglect, in *Unilateral Neglect: Clinical and Experimental Studies*, (eds I.H. Robertson and J.C. Marshall), Laurence Erlbaum Associates, Hove.

Robertson, I.H. and North, N. (1992) Spatio-motor cueing in unilateral neglect. *Neuropsychologica*, **30**, 553–63.

Rothwell, N., Britton, P.G. and Woods, R.T. (1983) The effects of group living in a residential home for the elderly. *British Journal of Social Work*, **13**, 639–43.

Sparks, R. and Holland, A.L. (1976) Melodic Intonation Therapy for Aphasia. *Journal of Speech and Hearing Disorders*, **41**, 287–97.

Stokes, G. (1992) *On Being Old: The Psychology of Later Life*, Falmer Press, London.

Trexler, L.E. (1987) *Cognitive Rehabilitation: Conceptualization and Intervention*, Plenum Press, New York.

Twining, C. (1991) *The Memory Handbook*, Winslow Press, Oxford.

Ulatowska, H.K. (ed.) (1985) *The Ageing Brain: Communication in the Elderly*, Taylor and Francis, London/College Hill Press, San Diego.

Van Der Cammen, T.J.M., Simpson, J.M., Fraser, R.M. *et al.* (1987) The Memory Clinic: a new approach to the detection of dementia. *British Journal of Psychiatry*, **150**, 359–64.

Wilson, B.A. (1987) *Rehabiltation of Memory*, Guildford Press, New York.

Wilson, B.A. and Moffat, N. (1992) *Clinical Management of Memory Problems*, 2nd ed, Chapman & Hall, London.

7

Community care

Various remarks regarding community care have been made in this book. Criticisms of its mode of function are regularly made by Age Concern, Help the Aged, the Alzheimer's Disease Society as well as other agencies and such criticisms include:

- Too little preparation before implementation.
- Too little by way of available resources in the community to ensure satisfactory services.
- Discharge from hospital often made too early and lacking in appropriate support.
- Too few trained staff, usually as a result of too many redundancies.
- Lack of communication and understanding between Social and Health Services.
- Time and travel costs interfering with continued therapeutic approaches.
- Untrained staff often the only service support with the result that behaviours and symptoms are often overlooked or misunderstood.
- Home visiting services have little back-up, support or available resources and are unable to take responsibility for intervention without permission from senior officers who may also be inexperienced in the care of elderly people.
- Many day centres can prove unpopular and unhelpful as they may not offer any real stimulation and attendence can prove boring.
- Available support services – medical, psychological, community psychiatric nurses, occupational therapists, physiotherapists, chiropodists, etc. – are stretched to meet needs and as a result are unable to provide a satisfactory level of input.
- Many cases of need are missed, particularly early stages of difficulty, which could minimize later demands. There can be long waits for assessments and restrictive criteria for both assessments and services.
- Patients are faced with greater demands for payment, often beyond their means or resulting in a diminished standard of living. The cost of residential care may eventually exceed even the means of those with savings and could mean eviction from the home.
- There is considerable concern regarding other financial demands made on the person concerned and the relatives. In private homes special help from professionals may have to be paid for by the family, often resulting in lack of specialized, necessary professional input.

- Short stay or intermittent care beds are being cut with the result that patients may not receive a regular re-assessment and relatives are put under continued strain and may break down themselves.
- Some disabled elderly people are being denied help, or become one of the 12–20 clients a day on a home care staff member's list.
- For many years there was help available for cleaning, washing and practical home assistance. This has been stopped, or has to be paid for on a private basis, thus proving of little help for the poor and the disabled.
- There is no national standard for assessments. In many cases the assessment is minimal, lacking, for instance, any investigation of psychological aspects, cognitive changes or brain function.

It must be a major concern if patients are discharged from hospital without consideration and monitoring at home. In most cases this is routine practice, but errors can arise when patients with specific brain impairments are not seen by the specialist professions relevant to the situation. Such people may only be supported by relatives or care staff who not only lack the necessary information, but also have no notion of how to help.

It is extremely important that hospital staff know about the differing conditions that cause dementia and use appropriate strategies for the rehabilitation of individuals. To expect that untrained and uninformed home visitors take over care on discharge without guidance is courting disaster. Furthermore if a person is receiving home help without any recourse to NHS staff whatsoever, how can they be expected to recognize specific impairments, let alone know what to do?

General practitioners are expected to deal with all health problems, but they cannot be expected to be specialists in every field, so particular cases are referred to the relevant specialist. Health services for elderly people is also a specialist field and the GP can seek advice and help from geriatricians, psycho-geriatricians and psychologists. Unfortunately, many potential NHS patients may slip through the net in the early stages of a degenerative condition. Either the relatives fail to recognize the increasing difficulty, take over care themselves or home care workers fail to understand difficulties or are prevented from asking for a medical opinion as they are not in a responsible position to do so. The delay in the latter instance, due to reports taking time to reach and convince the necessary senior officers, may lead to more complications. The linkage between Social and Health Services leaves much to be desired.

A recent document produced by a group of psychologists outlined various aspects that required particular attention if care in the community was to succeed. It was stated that **all** people need:

- a social outlet – requiring friends with whom to converse;
- a group identity – providing a sense of belonging;

- a feeling of self-worth – recognized as a person in his or her own right;
- an occupation – something to do both physically and mentally;
- control – being in charge of his or her affairs and lifestyle;
- coping skills – either using well learned responses or learning new ones with the help of others, in order to cope with difficulties as they arise.

The group stressed the need for preventative measures so that problems could be solved or managed at an early stage, such as:

- at least an annual check-up by GP and practice nurse;
- an easily found resource/information centre providing explanations of recent government documents, updated information on legal matters, financial charges and exemptions, local societies and useful contacts, etc. (one centre could be an information booth in a local supermarket);
- research concentrated on the perceived needs of local elderly residents;
- the use of local radio, newspapers and religious organisations to pass on information;
- the help of active elderly people could be enlisted to run the resource centre or in putting their experience and knowledge at the disposal of professionals;
- in rural areas ensuring that certain professionals; e.g. a community psychiatric nurse, actually live in the area and are well known.

There is a need to make a contract which covers both sides – the provider and the receiver. Too often the professional person's perception of the problem takes precedence and the patient or client's wishes are ignored. Each person has rights and responsibilities, both must be recognized in order to ensure that the person has continued control over his or her life and that the service is properly supplied.

Risks are taken regularly by people, however once a person is regarded as impaired or disabled in some way the right to take a risk is deemed too dangerous. This leads to loss of control and over cautiousness on the part of carers. A person may not wish to eat a large amount, may want to go for a regular walk, risk falling or take other chances. To actively prevent the person needs very careful consideration as it could be interfering with his or her rights.

Community care forums should be held regularly in order to share views, provide feedback and discuss priorities; local people should have the right to be present or well represented. When an individual's degree of dementia is such that he or she is in conflict with professional opinion, negotiation or creative intervention should be employed.

As no one discipline has all the answers it is important that multi-disciplinary teams continue to operate. Co-operation and understanding between Social and Health Services should be addressed and improved.

Continuing care and respite beds must be protected and maintained, equally day hospitals and centres as well as 24 hour home care are important resources and must be available.

The services supplied by psychologists are not always understood and can often be overlooked or underused. Psychology services for elderly people offer:

- specialist assessment – cognitive, emotional, brain function, strengths and deficits;
- treatment, retraining programmes, management and counselling;
- training programmes for all levels of staff and all disciplines;
- help for staff in understanding and keeping the psychological needs of elderly people in view;
- advice on treatment, approaches to care, developments and plans;
- evaluation of services, environments and interventions;
- assistance with care plans, focusing on behavioural and emotional difficulties whilst making allowance for cognitive levels and experience.

A satisfactory assessment should involve the findings of a variety of disciplines: medical staff, occupational therapists, social workers, physiotherapists, nurses and speech therapists. The psychologist can provide information on:

- identifying the individual and that individual as part of a social system;
- relevant information from past history, present circumstances, environmental influences (including the persons therein) which might prove to be major factors in explaining difficulties, then finding answers to them;
- behavioural patterns both normal and abnormal;
- attitudes, values, coping skills, abilities, routines and habits and any breakdown in the person's normal system; the breakdown may be due to life events, physical illness, brain changes or damage, emotional trauma or chronic social or financial difficulties;
- identifying specific impairments of brain function causing odd behaviours and finding methods to retrain or modify the problems;
- examining the environment for possible influences or causes of the problems;
- drawing all the information together to find a suitable rehabilitative or management programme relevant to the individual;
- providing a follow-up system, even in the community, to ensure that the programme is understood by all concerned and implemented.

On discharge from hospital careful planning is required. A multidisciplinary team should discuss the appropriate placement, the necessary information required by the future carers and methods to monitor progress and maintain a good lifestyle. Relatives and the individual concerned should be included in the discussion and their opinions should be given every consideration.

While the medical model is of great importance, it should not be the only basis for care programmes. Emotional, environmental and psychological needs may have little relevance in the medical model, but are of supreme importance to an individual. The rehabilitative, retraining and management programmes that are required in order to assist a person or carers to maintain as normal a lifestyle as possible will include the medical profession as an essential part of a multi-disciplinary team, but the other disciplines have a major role to play too. It is vital that these other needs and disciplines are given equal concern in future planning and development or else the number of dependent elderly and disabled people will grow to such an extent as to be unmanageable, causing unnecessary stress to relatives and carers alike – not to mention the patient.

Although there are a multiplicity of answers yet to be found, there is sufficient knowledge in the hands of a variety of disciplines to enable successful programmes to be provided which will encourage independence, assist improvement and minimize stress. Cost effectiveness becomes a ludicrous term when it is applied solely to the cost of basic care and neglects to estimate the long term cost of dependency resulting from inadequate provision in the initial stages. In the present era, unless management becomes fully conversant with the real service requirements there is little hope for such provision. Management training should also include courses focusing on care aspects as it is impossible to apply industrial and profit-making techniques to human physical and psychological needs. One day any one of us could require help and if the cost cutting planning has resulted in the demise of relevant services, there will be no one there to answer the cries for assistance.

FURTHER READING

Age Concern (1993) *No Time To Lose*, London.

Age Concern (1993) *Briefings*, London.

Alzheimer's Disease Society (1993) *NHS Continuing Care Beds*, London.

Holden, U.P., Caulfalik, H., Little, A. and Stokes, G. (1995) *A Guide to Positive Psychological Care for Elderly People in the Community*, document produced for Psychologists' Special Interest Group in the Elderly (PSIGE).

Definitions

Akinesis – slowing of movement, delay in initiating movement of limb contralateral to a lesion
Bradykinesis – slowness in initiating voluntary movement, often seen in Parkinson's disease with accompanying mask-like faces due to poverty of movement of the facial muscles
Contralateral – the opposite side
Echolalia – echoing previous words
Extrapyramidal signs – Limb rigidity, cogwheel phenomena (muscles respond to tension in a series of jerks), limb tremor, hyperkinesia (too much movement)
Hyperkinesia – too much movement
Hypersomnia – excessive sleeping
Hypokinesis – a decrease in the amount of movement
Hypotension – low blood pressure
Infarct – death of tissue due to prolonged ischaemia
Ipsilateral – same side
Ischaemia – impairment of blood supply to the brain
Leukoaraiosis – leuko = white; araiaosis = reduced density, therefore – reduced density of white matter
Myoclonus – jerky movements
Neurones – brain cells
Neurotransmitters – chemical substances which are released from one nerve ending and passed to another via the gap between (synapse) in order to transmit impulses
Occlusion – obstruction
Paraphasia – errors in word usage, e.g. substitutions for the correct word ('I drove home in my pen' instead of 'car'), substituted syllables ('far' for 'car', or neologisms – new words ('I drove home in my dugly')
Praxis – movement
Pseudobulbar palsy – impairments of facial movements, dysarthria, dysphagia, upper motor neurone problems, possibly hemiparesis and short step gait
Pyramidal signs – spasticity, increased sudden reflexes, limb tremor, hyperkinesia (too much movement)

Subdural haematoma – blood clot caused by rupture of veins beneath the dura in the brain
Syncope/syncopal attack – brief loss of consciousness due to impairment of cerebral circulation

Hyperventilation guidelines

(1) Explain overbreathing. Point out that athletes and singers are taught to breathe from the thorax and often forget to breathe normally at other times. Activities which demand heavy, deep intakes of breath will use up the excess CO_2, so when running, climbing stairs, picking up heavy objects or even living at high altitudes, it is natural to breathe fast. However, the body cannot cope with this type of breathing in normal conditions. The rate, depth and nature of breathing change throughout the day, under stress the speed increases. Normal breathing is at about the rate of 10 breaths a minute, sometimes one or two less and sometimes one or two more.

A well known saying 'Take a deep breath' is not good advice. If a deep breath is taken, it must be exhaled slowly, or it could provoke the problems associated with hyperventilation.

The explanations are very necessary as it is difficult for a person with worrying symptoms to accept that they are caused simply by overbreathing.

(2) The person is asked to mentally count each normal breath whilst the therapist silently times a minute. This may need careful explanation to ensure that it is understood that a breath consists of both inhalation and exhalation. Anything over 12 breaths in a minute indicates some degree of unsatisfactory breathing.

(3) To demonstrate the difference between thoracic and diaphragmatic breathing the person should lie down and place a book on their stomach. If it moves up and down breathing is correct and the right muscles are in use. If it does not move, but the chest obviously does, then breathing is thoracic.

PRACTICE METHODS

Depending on the needs of the person, one or more of the following can be used.

Second hand

Either the second hand on a watch or, preferably, a wall clock can provide the timing. There are 12 numbers on a clock face, each number represents minutes, but also 5 seconds. If one full breath is taken every 5 seconds, the rate in a minute will be 12. This may be too fast too soon; if normal breathing has been over 20 breaths a minute the aim should be staged as follows:

$1^1/_2$ full breaths to each 5 seconds	= 18 in a minute
8 full breaths to each 30 seconds	= 16 in a minute
1 full breath to each 5 seconds	= 12 in a minute
1 full breath to each 6 seconds	= 10 in a minute.

The breathing should be slow, easy and shallow. 12 is a good rate for most older people. To reach that rate, depending on the number of breaths presently taken, one stage should be practised several times a day for 5 minutes over a week before the next stage is attempted – if there is one.

Mental strategy

If no clock with a second hand is available, if a mental check whilst outside the home is necessary or if blindness or visual difficulties are present another method can be used. This involves saying slowly, mentally, 'one thousand' for breathing in and 'two thousand' for breathing out. The rate can be slowed even further by saying, mentally, 'one thousand, two thousand' whilst breathing in and 'three thousand, four thousand' for breathing out.

Sometimes a person can experience gagging or sickness whilst trying to slow breathing down. The exercise should stop and a deep breath should be taken, though the breath must then be exhaled **very slowly**. A couple of swallows will help too. After this some pleasant thoughts, playing music or watching an amusing TV programme will be of assistance. The exercises can be resumed at a later time.

If a person suffers from dysphasia and does not understand, distraction can help. There is nothing odd or particularily strange about hyperventilation; perfectly fit, normal people can experience it.

Suggested guidelines for communication difficulties

These are a few ideas which can help with particular language difficulties.

The correct word for objects, people, etc., may be hard to find and there may be difficulties with reading or writing as well. This does not imply that the person's ability and intelligence is totally lost, indeed, apart from communication problems, these may not be damaged at all.

Communication is a two-way process:

- avoid talking as though the person was not there;
- encourage a response – use a notepad, ask the person to gesture, use pictures or written words;
- be patient and understanding, reinforce effort;
- keep conversation clear, simple and to the point;
- employ definite topics – people he or she knows, remembered places, events, interests;
- if frustration is apparent, leave things alone for a while;
- when speech is attempted refrain from supplying the word, use cues instead;
- sound the beginning of a word, or associate the word with a phrase, e.g. 'cup of ...'; 'You want your ...' or use examples, e.g. 'It has bristles', 'You clean your teeth with it';
- talk normally even if response is impossible or witheld;
- the **way** you speak will be understood, even if all you say is not;
- understanding may be damaged, but tone, emphasis, rhythm and gesture are probably preserved;
- aids such as teeth, glasses and hearing aids should be clean, in use and in working order.

To provide practice with language, some ideas are discussed: Grandchildren can be very helpful. Older people do not feel as threatened by playing simple games with children as they would with other adults. Memory and word games will stimulate thought and provide practice with word finding and usage. 'Fish' with pictures and words, 'Kim's game' with objects, pictures or words, card games, even 'I spy' are all possible aids. Many Bingo games can be devised which match words and sentences to pictures showing opposites, occupations, places or famous people. One word or sentence is on the Bingo card, and the matching one is on the card to be drawn out of the pile.

Recall of words can be encouraged by using pictures with large print for words such as 'saucepan', 'cutlery', 'pantry', 'linen'. These can be stuck on the correct cupboard or drawn throughout the house, especially in the person's own room. When an object is used, encourage attempts to name it, draw attention to the printed word, perhaps prompt or use repetition; also encourage the person to try to talk about routine tasks, e.g. dressing, when items could be named as they are put on. The association of action, objects and words related to these and, where possible, the written word, will provide practice and further understanding of the words being used.

When outside, point out the road signs, advertizing notices and shop signs. Read them aloud and encourage reading. In shops look at labels and prices, see if simple amounts can be added up so that the correct money and change can be estimated.

When errors occur correct **gently**, not making failure too obvious, but always praise and reinforce the successes.

Index

For Product Safety Concerns and Information please contact our EU
representative GPSR@taylorandfrancis.com
Taylor & Francis Verlag GmbH, Kaufingerstraße 24, 80331 München, Germany

www.ingramcontent.com/pod-product-compliance
Lightning Source LLC
Chambersburg PA
CBHW050519280326
41932CB00014B/2375

* 9 7 8 1 0 3 2 7 2 5 4 1 3 *